Gratitude

Thank you to all of the people on this planet I have met and those I am yet to meet.

Gary & Dain – for the amazing life changing tools from Access Consciousness and your friendship and empowering me to know that anything is possible.

Justine my PR agent – for always saying when something is not turning out so great, "Don't worry, it's just good copy!"

Moira – for changing my paradigms, when you asked me, "Why can't you have a house in Brisbane and the Sunshine Coast?"

Brendon – for being my enjoyable other, a daily inspiration, always seeing me and being the CFO of what we are creating together.

Rebecca, Amanda & Marnie – it could not have been created without your assistance. Thank YOU.

Joy of Business & Access Consciousness – thanks for having my back and being so incredibly creative and so much fun to play/work with!

Steve & Chutisa – thanks for all of our Financial 101 create times together!

Chris, Chutisa, Steve, Brendon, Gary & Dain – thank you for your stories of change that show people there is always a different possibility.

Don't give up. Don't quit. Keep creating and KNOW that anything is possible.

www.gettingoutofdebtjoyfully.com

Foreword

I was $187,000 in debt before I was willing to change my financial reality. That is a lot of money, and I pretty much had nothing to show for it! I had lots of different jobs and travelled all over the world. I had started businesses and I was having a lot of fun. I was still making money, but I didn't have a house or investments or any awareness of how much debt I was really in. I avoided looking at it, and in the back of my mind, I thought that maybe it would take care of itself!

In July 2002, I met Gary Douglas, the founder of Access Consciousness® (the company for which I am currently World-Wide Coordinator), at a Mind, Body and Spirit festival where I was running a stall for a business I had at the time, called "Good Vibes For You." A mutual friend brought Gary by to say hello. Gary gave me a hug and I pulled back straight away. He said to me, "You know, you'd be a lot better off if you were open to receiving. You'd be happier and you would make more money too." I thought he was crazy. What did he mean, receiving? It didn't make sense. I thought I had to give and give, and that's what would make my life work better. No one ever said anything about receiving! I thought I was here on this planet to *give*.

I went to one of Gary's talks at the festival. It was about relationships. He was real, he swore, he was irreverent, he was funny, and he wasn't telling people what they should and should not do. He was the first person who said that you can choose what works for you, you do not have to be or do what anyone else thinks you should. He said that you are the only one who knows what is true for you, nobody else. That was a totally different and totally empowering point of view. I was intrigued.

I began using a lot of the tools of Access Consciousness, and I noticed that my life started changing in miraculous ways. I became happier, and all kinds of things in life got easier and more joyful.

I listened to Gary and his business partner, Dr. Dain Heer, talk about Access Consciousness money tools a few times, but honestly, I did not really take in what they were saying or give it very much attention. It wasn't until my third Access class that I finally listened to what they were saying about money and the tools you can use to change your financial situation. I asked myself, "What would happen if I actually used these tools?" All these other parts of my life were changing when I applied the tools from Access, so perhaps my money situation could change too?

I did not tell anyone I was going to use the tools because I figured it would be the way it was when I gave up smoking. No one had really supported me. And how many people actually support you to make massive amounts of money anyway? So, just for me, I started using some of the tools, and my money situation began to change quite quickly. Money started to show up from seemingly random places and my willingness to *receive* money increased dynamically to the point that I could actually *have* the money that came in, rather than always having to find ways to spend it or pay it out as soon as it showed up. Hmmm—that "receiving" word again. Maybe Gary was onto something when he suggested I be open to receiving after all!

Within two years, I was out of debt.

You might expect me to say that it felt wonderful to be free of debt, but that wasn't so for me. I felt strange not having debt. I was more comfortable being *in* debt than *out* of debt. For one thing, it felt more familiar. It also matched the energy of the majority of my friends. And it definitely matched the energy of this reality, where everyone "knows" you are supposed to struggle for and with money. The general belief is that you have to work hard for your money. Money is not supposed to show up with ease and joy and glory. In light of all that, it is not so surprising that within a short time (about two weeks) I was in debt again. Luckily, I was willing to recognise what I was doing. I chose to be aware of what I was creating, and using the tools I had learnt in Access, I was finally able to truly turn my money situation around.

In this book, I am going to share with you the processes and tools I used to move from choosing debt to operating from a space of being willing to have money and use money to joyfully contribute to the expansion of my life and living. *This book is really about creating a financial reality that is joyful and works for you.* If you think you might like to do this, you have to be willing to be brutally honest with yourself and make different choices. You have to become adamantly clear about what you *would* actually like to choose because the truth is: *you* are the one that creates everything that shows up in your life.

It may be easy to think I am just spouting a well-worn platitude— "You can change anything!" — and you might be tempted to just gloss over it or dismiss it, but take another look at what I am suggesting: if you desire to create a financial reality that you truly love and truly works for you, you must acknowledge that *you* are the only person who can change things in your life, no one else. This doesn't mean you are all alone in the world and no one or nothing can help you or contribute to you. What it does mean is that you have to be willing to acknowledge that everything that has shown up in your life is there because *you created it being there.* Most people don't want to hear this, because they think it means they have to judge what they currently don't like about their lives even more than they already do. Please don't do that! Please don't judge you! You are not wrong. What you are is an amazing, phenomenal creator. Recognising that you are the creator of your entire reality is empowering - because if you created it, all of it, you can change all of it too. And it doesn't have to be anywhere near as difficult, or impossible as you think. You do, however, have to become clearer on what you would like to create as your financial world - and then use the tools that will work to help you create it. And that is why I wrote this book - to give you the tools, the questions and invite you to create whatever it is that you desire to have.

If you could change anything, if you could create anything in your financial world, what would you choose?

A special note: All of the tools in this book are from Access Consciousness; the stories are mine. A huge thank you to Gary Douglas and Dr Dain Heer for always being a contribution and a never-ending source of change.

Contents

PART ONE: NEW FINANCIAL REALITY 101 13

Chapter 1: What Makes Money? 15

    It Never Shows Up How You Think It Will (AKA the Myth of
    Cause and Effect) 16

    Ask And You Shall Receive 19

    Money Follows Joy, Not The Other Way Around 22

    "What brings you joy?" 24

    Stop Making Money Significant 26

Chapter 2: What Changes Debt? 29

    Your Point of View Creates Your (Financial) Reality 30

    Giving Up Comfort With Debt 34

    Be Willing to HAVE Money 37

    So what is having money? 38

    Stop Avoiding and Refusing Money 41

    Gratitude 44

Chapter 3: How Do You Create a New Financial Reality, Right Away? .. 49

    Being Willing to Do Whatever It Takes 51

    Giving up Your Logical and Insane Reasons for Not Having Money ... 56

    Being Brutally Honest With You (Kinder Than It Sounds) 59

    Trusting That You Know 64

PART TWO: MONEY COME, MONEY COME, MONEY COME! 67

Chapter 4: Ten Things That Will Make The Money Come
(And Come And Come) 69

Chapter 5: Ask Questions that Invite Money 71

Chapter 6: Know Exactly How Much Money You Need to Live - Joyfully! 75

Chapter 7: Have Money 79

Tool #1 For Having Money: The 10% Account.........................80

Tool #2 For Having Money: Carry Around The Amount of Cash
You Think a Rich Person Would Carry 82

Tool #3 For Having Money: Buy Things of Intrinsic Value............83

Chapter 8: Acknowledge You 85

Chapter 9: Do What You Love 91

Chapter 10: Be Aware of What You Say, Think and Do 97

Chapter 11: Stop Being Vested in the Outcome 103

Chapter 12: Give Up Believing in Success, Failure, Need's & Wants.... 107

Chapter 13: Have and Be Allowance 113

Chapter 14: Be Willing To Be Out Of Control 117

Chapter 15: A Note About Cash-flow 121

PART THREE: SUMMARY AND TOOLS..............................125

Summary of Chapters, Questions and Tools.......................126

Two More Access Consciousness Tools You Can Add To
Exponentialise Everything 158

The Access Consciousness® Clearing Statement..............................159

Right and Wrong, Good and Bad 160

How The Clearing Statement Works 162

How to Use The Clearing Statement 163

Access Bars® 164

Access Consciousness Money Processes...........................165

PART FOUR: STORIES OF CHANGE 171

Stories of Change..173

Interview with Christopher Hughes.................................174

Interview with Chutisa Bowman and Steve Bowman.......................186

Interview with Brendon Watt..200

Interview with Gary Douglas 213

Interview with Dr Dain Heer 230

Part One

New Financial Reality 101

Chapter 1

What Makes Money?

If you are looking for a quick fix to your money problems, this isn't it.

If you are looking for something that will give you the perspectives and tools to change your entire lifestyle, your reality and future with money, and you are willing to give yourself at least 12 months and see what can be created in that time, this book will have a lot to contribute to you.

What I would really like you to get is that you are the source for the creation of money in your life. When you are willing to be everything that you are, you become an infinitely creative source for everything in your life - including money. You have an unlimited (and mostly un-accessed) capacity to create a financial reality that would work for you. The problem is, most of us have been taught so many things about money that simply are not true. When we begin to unpack those myths and misconceptions, and start to play with different perspectives and combine them with simple and pragmatic tools, dynamic change in your monetary world becomes a lot easier and more joyful to create.

What if money is not what you have bought, been told, sold or taught that it is? What if your willingness to be curious, questioning, playful, and to receive the random, unexpected and unpredictable could make you way more money than you ever imagined?

Are you willing to have the adventure of creating a life and living with lots of money in it? Truth? Did you answer "Yes"? Then, let's get started!

IT NEVER SHOWS UP HOW YOU THINK IT WILL (AKA THE MYTH OF CAUSE AND EFFECT)

Most people believe that finance and money is a linear thing. We are told over and over, "In order to make money you have to do and be A, then B, then C." That is the mindset we come to live by and we spend our time constantly searching for the perfect formula for making lots of money. We keep looking at money as something that only shows up as a result of doing certain things (like working hard, working many hours, inheriting money or winning the lottery). But what if creating money was not necessarily a cause and effect paradigm? What if money could show up in all kinds of ways, from all kinds of places?

When I changed my financial reality, I had money show up in the most bizarre places. Money was gifted to me, and I had really odd and lucrative jobs show up. It was also a lot easier for me to recognise and receive these different things showing up because at that point I was asking, "What are the myriad of different ways money can show up for me now?" and I was willing to do anything and take any job that was adding to my life and expanding my financial reality. I didn't refuse the money or the possibilities. Rather, I opened up to them, with no point of view of what they looked like. This allowed things to show up and contribute to my life in ways I wouldn't have been able to even recognise if I had decided money had to come into my life in an "A, B, C" linear-type fashion.

What if you could be the strange person that changes your reality around money and finance forever by giving up your linear points of view around money? What if you could have unlimited revenue streams? What if you can create money in ways no one else can? Are you willing to give up having to compute, define or calculate *how* money will show up and allow it to come into your life in random, magical and miraculous ways? No matter what it looks like? Even if it looks *totally* different from anything you have ever considered?

"Give up asking to manifest things, and let the universe do its job!"

Once upon a time, I was a bit of a hippie. I loved all the spiritual stuff. I would get upset if I forgot to cleanse my crystals under the full moon. My friends and I would talk about what we would like to "manifest" in our lives. Imagine my surprise when I met Gary Douglas and he explained that "Manifesting is the 'how' of things showing up - and how something shows up is the universe's job. It's your job to actualise: it's your job to ask for it and be willing to receive it, *however* it shows up."

Confused? Ok, let's look at this a little closer. *Manifest actually means, "How it shows up". When you say to the universe, "I would like to manifest this," you are saying, "I would like to how it shows up this," which doesn't make any sense. It's confusing and unclear for the universe and so it can't deliver. The universe desires to contribute to you, you can ask it for anything! But when you do, be clear and ask for something to show up in your life, not how it shows up. Ask, "What would it take for this to show up? What would it take to actualise this in my life right away?" Basically, if you desire for the universe to assist you, ask for WHAT you want, not HOW you want it, and that means giving up asking to "manifest" things. Create more clarity between you and the universe - start asking for things to actualize and to show up in your life, and let the universe take care of the "how".*

How much time do you spend trying to handle the "how" of things showing up in your life?

How much time do you waste your energy and effort trying to line things up and control certain outcomes into existence? How much time do you spend desperately trying to figure out *how* and *when* it's all going to come about, rather than ask for it and just be willing to recognise it and receive it when it does? The universe has an infinite capacity to manifest, and it usually has a much grander and magical way of doing it than you can predict. Would you be willing to give up all your considerations of how something has to show up and let the universe do its job unhindered? All you have to do is to receive, and stop judging you.

You have to be willing to stop trying to control, predict or figure out how (and when) money will show up and be willing to actualise it. To actualise with greater ease, you have to take your blinkers and blinders off and open up to the myriad of ways the universe desires to gift to you, so you will not miss it when it does.

Sometimes the universe has to move things around in order to create what you desire. It might not happen right away, but that doesn't mean nothing is happening! Don't judge that it can't or won't show up, and don't judge yourself that you are doing something wrong, or it will stop what you started when you asked for what you desire. Be patient and don't limit the future possibilities.

Remember: "Demand of yourself, and request of the universe."

"Money isn't just cash."

Gary often tells a story about a lady that came to one of his money classes. A few weeks later he rang her up to see how she was doing and she said, "Nothing has changed, this didn't work for me!" He asked her why she thought that and she said, "Because my bank balance is the same as it was before." Gary asked her what else had been going on recently. She told him, "Oh well, a friend of mine bought a new car and gave away her current car to me for free. Another friend gave me her whole designer wardrobe that she has never worn because she doesn't want it anymore, and I am currently living right on the beach in this really nice condo rent-free while that same friend is overseas for 6 months."

Gary said to the woman, "You have a new car, a new wardrobe and an amazing place to live - and you think nothing has changed! You have just received thousands of dollars worth of things in the last few weeks! How is that *not* more money in your life?" The woman had only been open to seeing the money in her life as cash in the bank. But how much would it have cost her to buy a car, a designer wardrobe or to pay rent where she was living?

There are so many ways that money and cash-flows can come into your life, but if you are not willing to acknowledge them, if you think they have to look a certain way, you are going to think you are not changing things, when, in fact, you are. What if you were willing to have all the ways that money can show up into your life, and more?

Are you willing to give up predicting, controlling and working it out and go on the journey of asking for what you truly desire to have as your financial reality, and receive the adventure of it showing up in ways you cannot currently imagine?

If so, it's time to look at another essential tool for creating money: asking and receiving.

ASK AND YOU SHALL RECEIVE

People make judgements and statements about money all the time, but very few ask questions about it.

If you are like just about everybody on the planet, you tend to judge yourself about the amount of money you have and don't have. The funny thing is, it doesn't matter whether you have a lot of money or a little - most people have tonnes and tonnes of judgements around money. Regardless of what is in their bank account, very few people actually have a sense of ease and peace and abundance with money.

You might have heard the saying, "Ask and you shall receive." Have you ever truly asked for money? Have you ever truly been willing to receive it? Receiving is simply being willing to have infinite possibilities for something coming into your life, without a point of view about what, where, when, how or why it shows up. Your capacity to receive money opens up when you lose your judgements of money, and of you in relationship to money.

If you truly desire to change your financial reality, giving up judgement is going to have to be one of your primary steps in the process. Contrary to what the world tells us, judgements do not create more in your life. They keep you trapped in a polarised world of right and wrong, good and bad, aligning and agreeing or resisting and reacting. Judgement does not give you any freedom, choice, or possibility for anything different beyond one side of the coin or the other. Judgement stops you asking and stops you from receiving. The antidote? CHOICE. You have to choose to stop yourself in that moment of judgement and make the demand of yourself that you will no longer judge or go to some limited thought or conclusion. And then, ask a question.

Let's go back to this concept of being linear with money for a minute. When you believe, based on a bunch of thoughts, feelings, judgements and conclusions, that money can only show up in certain ways, then money cannot show up in any other way than what you have decided is possible or likely. With each judgement of what you have decided is not possible, you blind yourself to anything that could show up beyond your limited viewpoint; just like the lady Gary spoke to, who had created all this stuff worth a lot of money coming into her life, but decided nothing had changed because her bank balance was the same. If you are willing to let go of your judgements around money, you can begin to see possibilities that you previously considered impossible in your life, and invite more and more to come to you.

And one of the simplest ways to invite money into your life, is to ask!

Generally, I have noticed that people are not very good at asking for things. If you look at a little kid, they are naturally very curious, they want to know about things, and they tend to ask a lot of questions. And a lot of the time, this is discouraged.

When I was a kid, I was discouraged from talking about business or money at the dinner table, as my mother was raised to believe it was not good manners to do so. I was always curious about business and money and my father and brother were both accountants and they both loved business. I wanted to ask questions all the time, especially at the dinner table when we were all together, but I wasn't allowed because it was considered not appropriate.

Have you been taught that it's not proper, or that it is uncouth to talk about money? Have you been taught that it is wrong to ask about money? Have you been discouraged to ask questions at all?

I know so many people who were criticized for their curiosity from a young age. I have a friend whose mother once taped up his mouth to get him to stop talking because he asked too many questions! Another friend, whenever he asked questions as a kid, his family would say to him, "Curiosity killed the cat, can it please kill you?"

In truth, most people on the planet have been taught that asking for money, or asking for anything is something that you shouldn't really do, unless you have a really good reason or justification, like you have worked hard enough or can prove that you deserve it.

Years ago my fabulous reason for having money was, "I should have lots of money because I will do good things with it. I will use it to help people." Now there's nothing wrong with that idea essentially, but what it meant was that with every bit of money that came into my life, I couldn't allow it to contribute to my own life. I wasn't in the equation of people who I could help with it. This basically meant that anytime I received any money, I had to get rid of it. I couldn't have it in my life, or let it contribute to me directly, because I had to be helping other people all the time. The funny thing is, once I allowed myself to have money, to really have it in my life and let it contribute to my life, to enjoy it, and to enjoy being me, my ability to contribute to others increased— and continues to increase— exponentially.

Here's the thing: money does not have a point of view, it does not have a moral compass that says, "You have been good, so you can have more money," or "You have been bad, so no money for you!" Money doesn't judge. Money shows up to people who ask and are willing to receive it.

Take a look at the world - have you noticed that there are kind and unkind people with money and kind and unkind people without money?

You don't have to prove that you are good or bad, or that you deserve money, you have to be willing to stop judging whether you deserve money and ask for it, just because you can. Just because it's fun to have money!

What if you could ask for money, just because you know life might be more fun with it than without it? What if the purpose of your life is to have fun? Are you?

MONEY FOLLOWS JOY, NOT THE OTHER WAY AROUND

A lot of people ask me about how they can create more money in their life. I've talked with people who earn a set wage every month or every week as well as those who create other ways to bring in their money, where the amount varies from week to week or month to month. Regardless of their situation, I tell people that bringing in more money is about the *generative* energy you create.

A more simple way of saying this has been elegantly stated in this quote by Dr. Dain Heer: "*Money follows joy; joy doesn't follow money.*"

Sometimes I hear people say, "When I have x amount of money, I'll be happy or peaceful or at ease." What if you just woke up happy? What if you just had peace? What if you just had ease? What if you just started being a different energy, right now? The kind of energy that invites money into your life?

"If your life was a party, would money want to come?"

If you looked at your current life as a party, what kind of invitation would it be to money?

"Well... I am having this party, but we are not having any fun. We don't have nice food or drinks, we aren't going to wear nice clothes, and when you show up I am probably going to complain that you are not enough for me, that you are never around for long, and how upset I feel every time I think about you. And when you leave, I am going to judge you for that too, instead of being grateful that you came at all. Oh and I am going to bitch about you behind your back constantly."

If you got an invitation to a party like that, would you want to go?

If you were invited to a party where the host said, "Wow, I am so grateful you are here, thank you for coming!" There was awesome food, great champagne, music, people who were genuinely enjoying themselves and enjoying *you*, who didn't judge you for leaving the party, but invited you to come back anytime bringing as many friends with you as you'd like - might that be more the kind of party money would be enthusiastic about?

What if you started living your life as the celebration it can be, today? What if you did not wait for the money to show up? What if you started doing and being what brings you joy, right now?

"WHAT BRINGS YOU JOY?"

The energy you create when you're having fun, when you are totally, happily engaged in something you love, is generative. It doesn't matter how you create that energy. It doesn't have to be directly related to what you do that currently makes money (remember, we are giving up linear and cause and effect). Generative energy (the energy of joy) contributes to your life and your business, no matter when, how, where and why you create it, or what you create it with.

We don't really get asked to know what brings us joy and then seek out the innumerable ways we can make money from the fun of it - so it may take some time to get clear on what does bring you joy. Would you be willing to start asking yourself anyway, and choose whatever it is?

My partner Brendon became a "tradie" (that's Australian slang for a tradesman) at a really young age. He was a tiler. For so long Brendon believed tiling was the only thing he could really do in life, even though in truth he had the capacity for so much more. When we first started seeing each other, he really didn't get much joy out of being a tiler. So I allowed him the space to ask himself what really did bring him joy and to choose something different. I fully supported Brendon and his son financially for 18 months. I could see his capacities, and I could also see that he needed the space to make some choices about what he desired to do with his life. In that time he became more and more himself. He discovered more about what he is great at and what was joyful for him, whether that's cooking amazing meals, designing and undertaking home renovations, playing in the stock market or investing in property. If he had been caught up in the idea that he had to remain a tiler for the rest of his life, he never would have allowed himself that change.

What if you could allow anyone (even you) the space to choose something different? No matter how old you are, no matter how long it takes, and no matter if you have no idea where to start?

If you are 55 and you ask yourself this question and you go, "I always really wanted to be in the circus," — be in the circus! Do whatever it is you would love to do because it will bring you more money. Do not create anything as a justification for why you are not choosing something.

"Your life is your business, your business is your life!"

What do you love to do, just for fun? What if you would do this for one hour a day and one day a week?

I have this saying: "Your life is your business, your business is your life." What if the business of living was the business you are really in, no matter what you actually did for a job? What energy are you running your life with? Are you having any fun?

I often take my dog for a walk on the beach in the morning. Every time we go, it's like the first time ever for him. He bounds around with exuberant energy as if to say, "This is awesome! This is amazing!" He runs along the beach and into the ocean and has a great time. For me, it's often when I am just enjoying the beach and being with my dog that I get my best creative and generative ideas. Creating that space for joy is a contribution to ourselves that we do not acknowledge nearly enough.

No amount of money in the world can create happiness. You create it. By doing what you enjoy doing. By being YOU. So please, start doing and being whatever it is you truly desire to do and be. Start being happy. Just start.

If you desire to have more money in your life, you have to be willing to have a really good time. No matter what it takes, no matter what it looks like and no matter how it shows up, because it never shows up how you think it will.

You have to be willing to have joy, and allow the money to follow.

STOP MAKING MONEY SIGNIFICANT

What does money mean to you? Does it have a lot of significance in your life? What emotions do you have around money? Joy, happiness, ease? Anxiety, stress and difficulty?

Anything we make significant and meaningful becomes a source for judgement of ourselves, and of the thing we have made significant.

When you give something significance, you make it greater and more powerful than you are. Anything that has significance in your life, you make *it* the powerful thing, and *you* become the powerless victim. It's not actually true that it is greater, or that you are powerless, but what you do is you make it so important and significant to you in your life that you decide you cannot live without it, and you make yourself choiceless in regards to it - except for doing whatever it takes to hold onto it. The problem is when you hold onto something tightly, the life drains out of it. When you create significance around anything, you suffocate it and suffocate you so that there is no room for anything to grow, breathe, change or expand.

Have you also noticed that when you make something meaningful, important, or imperative it becomes practically impossible to feel playful, happy or at ease with it? It becomes impossible to truly create more of it in your life because you are too busy trying not to lose however much you currently have. That's exactly what we tend to do with money.

There is a *lot* of significance around money.

26

It may seem an impossible request to ask you to imagine your life with no significance around money, but look at it for a minute. If money were not significant, how much freedom would that give you? How much more choice? How much lighter and happier would you feel in all aspects of life?

What if you started today with creating every part of your life as a joyful celebration?

Many years ago, I realised that I had been getting stuck in a mindset of choosing everything that I could and could not do based on the money that I had in my bank account. I had been asking myself what it would take to create the money to go to Costa Rica for an Access Consciousness event. I remember this moment not long after, where I was sitting with a wad of cash I had created. I had the money right in my hand, but I was going to all these thoughts of what I should be doing with it and could be doing with it and worrying if more was going to show up or not. Someone had said to me around that time, "When are you going to stop making money more significant than you?" And when I looked down at the cash in my hand, I began to see it as all these beautiful colourful pieces of paper. I looked at it all, and I thought, "Wow, I am making this paper in my hand more significant than the choices I could make in my life? That's insane!" After that, I made the demand of myself that I am not making money worth more than me. What you have to remember is that money is not the source of creation, you are the source of creation. YOU create your life!

To create a joyful financial reality with money, you have to give up everything you decided was significant about money, and you have to be willing to be joyful and to be happy, with or without money. What if you began to create your life as an irresistible invitation to money to come play with you? What points of view about money would you have to lose in order to create that with ease?

Remember-

- Debt is a choice —

- You have a choice to get
  into

  of debt

- What else is possible

- What else can I do
  to change

What if I could
chose parking —?

What would I like
to create?

Chapter 2

What Changes Debt?

What is your point of view about debt? Does it seem normal, inevitable or unavoidable to you? Have you been taught to believe that debt is bad, wrong, or a necessary evil? Do you avoid looking at your debt? Do you keep yourself ignorant about debt, and hope that it will take care of itself?

What if I were to tell you that debt is just a choice? It's not good, it's not bad, it's not right or wrong - it's a choice.

This may sound simplistic, yet the most essential and powerful tool for getting out of debt is to recognise that debt is a choice you have, and that you can change it if you desire to do so. Once you make the choice to get out of debt, you can change everything.

Often when I say to people, "Debt is just a choice. Money is just a choice," they don't really want to know it. They would prefer to judge themselves rather than have a look at what they are currently creating as their reality.

You may ask yourself, "If debt is just a choice, why do I have it? What have I done wrong? Why haven't I gotten it right?" Please don't judge, blame or go into the wrongness of you. What if nothing you have ever been or done is wrong? It got you to this moment, seeking something different, reading this book and searching for other possibilities with money, right? So, what if now is the perfect time to choose something new?

And you can choose something new, right away. The moment you choose something different, you shift your reality with money. The moment you say to yourself, "You know what? No matter what, I am going to change this!" you empower yourself to begin taking off the debt-coloured glasses and ask, "What else is possible?"® and "What can I do to change this?"

How much have you created your life from a place of debt? What if instead of choosing from a point of view of, "I can't change this," you instead tapped into the question of, "What if I could choose anything? What if I chose for me? What would I like to create?"

When you change your point of view, your reality changes. What point of view do you have that is creating your current financial situation? What if you allowed yourself to change that point of view? Would it give you freedom to choose something different?

YOUR POINT OF VIEW CREATES YOUR (FINANCIAL) REALITY

What is the difference between what is real and what isn't real for you in life? Your choice on how you view it. The point of view you have had about money up until now has created your current money situation. How is that working for you?

From the moment we are conceived, we are absorbing our parents' reality, our community's reality, our friend's, our relative's, our peer's, our teacher's, our culture and our society's reality about money. We are constantly projected at and expected to buy into those same points of view. We are not taught to question if it is true, real or relevant to us. We are told, "That's just the way it is, this is the reality of the situation." But, what if it's not?

I could have bought my family's point of view that it was inappropriate to talk about money at the dinner table, and made myself wrong for desiring to talk about money over dinner. I could have stopped doing it. But what I did instead was recognise that their point of view was just their point of view and that it didn't have to be real and true for me. My partner and I love talking about money over a glass of wine and dinner. We have what we like to call 'Financial 101s' whilst enjoying the delicious meals he cooks. We talk about where we are at with money, what we would like to create with money one year, five years, ten years in the future and to play with the idea of what else is possible we haven't considered. We have fun, we generate a lot of enthusiasm and joy in our lives, we come up with great ideas, and we set new targets. If I had bought other people's points of view as true for me, I would not have been able to create this marvellous part of my reality that I enjoy with my partner and that contributes immensely to our lives and the creation of our finances.

If you "un-fixed" your fixed points of views of money, if you had no judgement of money, what would you create your financial reality to be? Would it be serious and problematic, like we are so often told it is? Or would you create something very, very different?

"Have you decided that the solid, heavy stuff in life is real?"

I spoke with a woman who wanted to expand her business, but she had concluded she wouldn't have enough money to survive if she went forward with her plan. She felt paralysed. She said she knew she was functioning from an energy that was not real or true, yet it somehow kept her inside a box. I asked her, "Are you making your conclusions real? There is a heaviness about them that we associate with this reality. But what if there's nothing to them? What if they are just an interesting point of view?"

The woman asked, "But isn't it real that I need money to pay my bills? Isn't it real that I need money to pay for my food? Isn't all of that real?"

I said, "Everyone is telling you, 'You have to pay your bills and you have to buy your food,' but those are conclusions. You don't have to do those things. You could go bankrupt. You could not pay your bills. You could just leave. You could drop in at a friend's house and eat their food. There are a million different things you could do. You could also choose to create something completely different." It really goes back to choice. You have choice. What are you choosing?

Many years ago, I was also having a difficult time, and I rang a friend. When I told him what was going on, he said, "Yeah, Simone, but that's not real." I was standing in my kitchen thinking, "It *is* real. This *is* real." I started laughing because I wanted so badly for this friend to buy into where I was functioning from. I wanted him to align and agree with my conclusions and limitations and say, "You know what? You're right, this one is real."

What have you decided is real and not real for you? Why have you decided it's real? Because that was your experience in the past? Because it "feels" real: heavy, solid, substantial or immovable? Would something that is true for you really feel like a tonne of bricks, or would it make you feel lighter and happier?

You look at something that is solid - like a brick or a building. Science has shown us that even the most solid things are actually 99.99% space. What if what you have decided is real, solid and immovable actually is not and it is just how you have been taught to see it? What could change if you chose to recognise that perhaps everything you think is so, isn't necessarily so?

*"A great tool for creating ease
with any point of view is to make it
interesting, rather than real."*

One of my favourite Access Consciousness tools is this: for the next three days, for every thought feeling and emotion that comes up (not just about money, but about everything) what if you would say to yourself, "Interesting point of view I have that point of view"? Say it a few times and notice if something changes. Let's try it out: What is your biggest problem with money right now? Get hold of that thought and any feeling or emotion that comes up with it. Now look at it and say, "Interesting point of view I have that point of view." Has anything changed? If not, say it again. Say it three more times, 10 more times. Notice anything different? Does it become harder to hold onto? Does it become less substantial and solid? When you stop buying into any point of view as real or absolute and see it as merely interesting - it starts to lighten up and have less impact in your universe. When you say, "Interesting point of view I have this point of view" to a thought, feeling or emotion, and it dissipates or changes, that means it really isn't true for you.

Now think of someone you are really grateful for in life. Get the energy of having them in your life, look at it and say, "Interesting point of view I have that point of view." Does that go away and dissipate? Or does something else happen?

When something is true for us, and we acknowledge it, it creates a sense of *lightness* and *expansiveness* in our world. When something isn't true, like a judgement or a conclusion we have come to about something, it is heavy, and it feels contracted or tight. When you say, "Interesting point of view I have this point of view," what is true for you expands and grows, and what is not becomes less substantial and dissipates.

Here's another way you can use "Interesting point of view" as you read through this book. For every thought, feeling or emotion that comes up for you around money as you read, take a minute to acknowledge that point of view, then use "Interesting point of view". You may find out that pretty much everything you thought was solid and absolute about your current financial situation is just interesting, and not at all real. With "Interesting point of view", everything becomes malleable. You get to choose whether you want to keep it, change it, or create a totally different point of view.

What would you like to create and choose today?

GIVING UP COMFORT WITH DEBT

I often talk with people who were in debt, became debt-free, and then went back into debt. I have done that myself. Recently, I talked with someone who said, "I was debt-free and had money in my bank account for the first time in my life, but I'm $25,000 in debt again. This is the fourth time! What is behind this pattern? I do not like being in debt or struggling to find money to pay back the debt, but I also don't like the restriction of not choosing something just because I don't have the money."

I asked her, "Are you truly willing to be debt free?" and she recognized that she could not actually answer, "Yes!" For her, there was something more comfortable about being *in* debt than *out* of it. I know that was true for me when I first got out of debt, and it may be true for you as well. I was actually disappointed when I first got out of debt. I thought, "Where are the trumpets and the fireworks and the big street parade going 'Yeah Simone, you are awesome!'?" It was a bit of a letdown. It felt strange and unfamiliar not having that debt in my life. For how many of you is that a familiar feeling too?

There are a lot of reasons we are more comfortable in debt than out of it. You may be accustomed to being like everyone else. You may not wish to be the tall poppy (this is a term we use in Australia to describe people of genuine merit who are resented, attacked, cut down, or criticised because their talents or achievements make them stand out from the crowd) or you may not like the idea of being judged for being the only person you know who doesn't have debt or money problems.

If you keep finding yourself in a certain amount of debt, and you truly wish to change it, you have to have the courage and confront yourself with what you are currently choosing and make a different choice. Are you willing to be uncomfortable in order to create freedom in this area? If so, let's do something a bit weird: let's look at what you actually *love* about being in debt.

"What do you love about being in debt and having no money?"

It may seem a strange question to ask, but when we have something going on in our lives that we say we hate, often there is something we secretly love about creating it that we are not looking at. If you are willing to ask some questions, you can acknowledge what is keeping you stuck. If you don't acknowledge it, you can't change it.

- What do you love about being in debt for that amount? Is that the amount of debt that is comfortable for you? Does it keep you stuck in a limited financial reality? Does it keep you the same as everybody else?

- What do you love about having no money? Does it make sure you don't stand out from your family members? If you had money, do you believe your family would demand you to give it to them?

- What do you love to hate about having no money? Does it give you something to complain about, a story or justification that you can fall back on, rather than just change it?

- What do you hate to love about having no money? Have you been told it's wrong to love money? Is money the 'root of all evil'? Do you judge your choice to have no money? Would you consider not judging you, and recognise you have a different choice now?

- What choice can you make today that can create more now and in the future?

You may not be very comfortable asking yourself these questions. You may be tempted to judge yourself more. Please don't. What if acknowledging all the crazy stuff we decided we loved about being in debt was really the key to changing it - by looking at it without judgement and realising that sometimes we are just cute and not so bright - and then acknowledging you can make a different choice? What if it's not wrong? What if you could be grateful for your courage to look at this?

I am going to tell you a story about one of my insane points of view about money and debt that I was using to keep me from having money. I love my Dad. He was a really kind man. He would often say that he would not die until he could make sure that his family had an education and were secure financially. Everything he did as a man was about creating a safe and secure life for his wife and children. I didn't want my Dad to die because I loved him so much. Now, my mother and siblings were all financially stable, and we had all received a good education. The only one who did not have it all together, was me. I realised that even though I was perfectly capable of creating a great financial future, I had created myself as a financial mess because I thought, "As long as I have debt and money problems, my Dad won't die." Now, looking at that logically, it's a pretty insane point of view, right? But that is what I had been doing. Luckily, my Dad was still alive at that point, and I talked to him about it. He said in his Lithuanian accent, "Ah Simone, that is crazy, what are you doing" and I said, "I know!" I began to change my debt

36

from that point onward. And I also got to see the joy and happiness in his world increase as I began to create a greater financial reality for myself. To put it simply, *I began to receive.*

Are you willing to be aware of what you would truly like your life to be like? Are you willing to go beyond your comfort zones with debt and money, and begin to thrive rather than just survive?

BE WILLING TO HAVE MONEY

A friend once told me, "I'm really good at creating no money. And when I do create and generate money, I have a false sense of wealthy living. I spend a lot. I have lots of debt to pay, but I am not making it a priority. Instead I spend money, the faster the better, and then I am back in the trap again. What is this and how can I change it?"

There are a lot of people like this. They like to *spend* money more than they like to *have* money. Do you enjoy having money? Or is spending the most important thing in your life? Do you always find somewhere to spend your money? Do you pay off your credit cards and think, "Great! I've got another $20,000 (or whatever your credit limit is) to spend"?

We have been taught that the value of having money is spending it, or saving it to spend later. But we rarely talk about *having* money, and what difference that can make in our financial worlds.

> *"There is a difference between having, spending, and saving money."*

Gary Douglas says that he always hires people who are willing to have money, whether or not they currently have it. He knows that those who are willing to have money (regardless if they currently have a lot of money or not) will make money for themselves and the business, but if they are not willing to have money, they won't.

It took me a while to be willing to actually have money. I was great at creating it. I had businesses that lost money and businesses that made money. I have always created money, no matter what, even when I was in debt. I could make it, save it and spend it too. The one thing I was not willing to do, however, was to educate myself about money. I thought ignorance was bliss. Sound familiar?

I once created a business overnight with a friend making jars of glitter gel to sell just so we could go to all the parties during Mardis Gras in Sydney. When I decided I wanted to go overseas, I worked hard, I had three jobs and saved up all my money so I could travel; and wherever I went, I worked all kinds of jobs so I could keep traveling. And yet, I didn't allow myself to truly *have* money.

I was not frugal, I would spend money on the things I enjoyed, I wouldn't say no to a weekend in Melbourne with friends, I would be generous and enjoyed buying things for other people too. I wasn't the kind of person you would hear complaining about my money situation either, but I still wasn't allowing myself to have money.

SO WHAT IS HAVING MONEY?

Having money is about being willing to allow money to be in your life in such a way that you always have it, and it contributes to the expansion of your life. It is not making it significant. It is playing with money and allowing contribution and the willingness to receive.

A great example of this is I used to wear bright costume jewellery. It looked great, I had some fun pieces, but they were worth less than 50% of what I paid for them the minute I walked out the door. One day, I bought a necklace that was made of Mabe pearls. These pearls are now extremely rare, as the ocean does not produce them anymore. The necklace, because of the intrinsic value and its rarity in the world, keeps increasing in value. Having that necklace in my life not only has a monetary value that is more than what I paid for it, it is also an amazing and beautiful piece of jewellery to have in my life. It is aesthetically beautiful, and I feel amazing when I wear it. That is the energy that having money in your life creates.

Having money in your life is not just about creating it and never spending it. When you are truly willing to have money in your life, you are also willing to use it so that you create more.

A friend I know is always trying to *save* money for the businesses he works with. He is brilliant with technology and was working with a big company, traveling with them, and taking care of their audio-visual needs wherever they went. After each event, he would pack the equipment, lug it to the next country and city, and it created a lot of work for him. At one point, the owner of the company said to him, "I want you to buy more equipment so we have it in Europe, America, Australia, and Asia. That way, we won't have to take it everywhere when we travel, and we will not have to think about it." Two years went by and he hadn't bought anything. No one realised it until one day when the owner said, "I asked you two years ago to get more equipment. What happened?"

He said, "I was trying to save you money because all the equipment is so expensive."

Have a look at the energy of trying to save money by lugging equipment around to all these countries. Then look at the energy of having equipment available in each country. Which energy is conducive to having the business grow and expand with ease?

Are you someone who asks, "How can I save money?" What's the energy of that question? Is there a generative energy in it? Does it seem

When y ou have money in your life you are willig to use it

to expand your choices, or limit them? Now, look at the energy of these question "What would it take to generate more money?" "What energy do I need to be to create it with ease?"

Is there somewhere you are trying to save money? Try asking: "If I spent this money I'm trying to save, would it create more for today and the future?" I'm not saying go out and get a new convertible BMW if you want one. I'm suggesting you have a look at what is going to generate more for you. If something is going to do that, then spend the money.

What would it be like to have money in your life that is there to contribute to you? What would it be like to have things in your life that are of intrinsic value and increase in value over time?

Imagine two houses: one that is furnished with everything from a cheap modern day furniture store. It is clean and modern and looks just like the catalogue, and everything is worth less than 50% of what you paid for it. The other house is furnished with all kinds of beautiful things - silver, crystal, antiques, paintings, furnishings - which not only have a unique and aesthetic value, but actually have the added bonus of being worth at least what you paid for it and more. Which house would create a greater sense of wealth and beauty in your life? What if you could use the creation of aesthetics and of having all kinds of things in your life in a way that added to you having more money, now and in the future? It is not about judgement, it is about awareness and creating a future that you desire to have.

Would you allow money to be in your life constantly, and for it to keep growing?

In Part Two of the book, I will give you a number of practical tools for having money in your life. Having money is actually quite simple. Are you willing to have money and let it contribute to you in a totally different way?

STOP AVOIDING AND REFUSING MONEY

Is there anywhere in your life that you refuse or avoid looking at your money situation? Do you have really good reasons to avoid doing simple and easy things to create more money? Every place where we avoid being totally honest, is where we cut off and refuse what would give us more possibilities and easy change.

I was talking with a client who said, "I think about my debt nearly every day, and then I push it behind me and hope it goes away." A lot of us operate this way.

When I was in debt, I persistently and consistently avoided looking at what was going on with my financial situation until I finally chose to listen to Gary and Dain and began to use the tools of Access Consciousness. Avoiding awareness with money never creates a place where you can look at the choices you really have, it always creates this vague and unclear area where you do not empower yourself to see what is going on or what you can do to change it.

A friend of mine is really brilliant with teaching her kids about money. One time she gave her 10 year old $20 for him and his friends to have lunch together. Later, she found out that the other kid's Mum ended up paying. My friend asked her kid why he didn't pay and he admitted that he had lost the money before he got there. She then asked him to please go tell the other mother that he was going to pay for the lunch but that he lost the money. She knew the mother didn't mind paying, it wasn't about making anyone wrong. It was about acknowledging what had occurred - not from having a point of view or a judgement about the situation, but from getting her child to acknowledge what he had created, rather than pretending it didn't happen. You have to acknowledge, not hide or avoid things. It's not about judging. If you are willing to not ignore it, you will be willing to be more aware in the future. And with that awareness, you empower yourself to make the choices

that you would truly like to make, that would create more in your life, and not less.

"Are you living in a 'No-Choice Universe?'"

For years I avoided relationship. I'd say, "I don't do relationship, I'm not doing relationship, I'm never getting married, I'm never having kids." I looked all around me and I couldn't see a relationship that seemed to work. I could not see people who looked like they were having fun in their relationship, so my point of view (conclusion) was, "I'm not doing relationship!"

With that decision, I was shutting out everything else that was possible. I was creating a no-choice universe and a no-choice reality. One day, I realised that's what I was choosing and I began to ask myself, "What if I were willing to be in a relationship? What if I were willing to receive that possibility?" I let go of everything I had decided and concluded about relationships, because I recognised that all those assumptions were creating huge limitations for me. Everywhere we go into conclusion, we create limitations, which separate us from the infinite possibilities that are available. The funny thing is, I do now have a relationship with a fabulous partner, and he came along with a child and a dog too - instant family. And they have all contributed to my life in ways I could never have imagined. If I had continued to refuse the possibility of relationship in my life, I could not have received the major contribution, generosity and energy they are to me, including contributing to creating more money and wealth.

What I am talking about here is looking at the energy that giving yourself choice creates in your life. When you avoid something, refuse or are unwilling to have something, it doesn't allow you to have more choices or create more. You have to be willing to look at where you are creating a no-choice universe, and be willing to change it.

"What's the worst that could happen if you didn't avoid money?"

Do you avoid doing new things that could make you money? How many situations have shown up where you could have made money and you said, "No, I don't have the time for that. I couldn't go there. I couldn't possibly do it"? Have you ever been asked to do something and you thought, "I don't have the capacity to do that," so you refused and avoided it rather than giving it a go? What if you had asked yourself, "What's the worst thing that could happen if I didn't avoid this and just chose?" Choice creates awareness.

If you were avoiding public speaking and you asked, "What is the worst thing that could happen if I actually did some public speaking?" You might ask, "Well, I could freeze up and forget what I was going to say. Would it really be that bad?" And then you might say, "If that happened, I could just stand there, look at the crowd, and smile." People love the vulnerability of you being you, and if you are not avoiding anything, it is easier to be you in any situation. You get to have more of you no matter what is going on, because you do not have to twist and turn or hide yourself to avoid anything. What will definitely create more money in your life, is you becoming more of you.

Are you avoiding your debt? Where are you avoiding money? What wonderful, great and creative parts of you are you refusing to have show up in the world with that avoidance? What have you decided is the worst thing that could happen if you did not avoid it? What could change if you were willing to have total awareness of your financial reality?

GRATITUDE

One of the most magical tools for changing things in life is gratitude.

Gratitude often gets overlooked, but it has the power to change your point of view dynamically. Gratitude has this natural effect of getting you out of judgement. Gratitude and judgement cannot co-exist. You cannot judge and have gratitude. Have you ever noticed how it is impossible to be grateful when you are judging something or someone? When you have gratitude, you come out of judgement. And as we have also previously discussed, judgement is how we create our greatest limitations.

When you receive money, what is your instantaneous point of view? Are you grateful for every dollar, every cent, that comes into your life or do you tend to think, "That's not much," "It will cover this bill," "I wish I had more"? What if whenever money came in, and whenever money went out, you were grateful - to you for creating it, to the money for showing up and for what you spend it on? What would it be like if you truly had more gratitude with money?

What if, for any money that comes in, you practiced saying, "Thank you, I am so glad this showed up! Can I have more please?" And what if, for any money you spent, and for every bill you paid, you were both grateful and willing to ask for more: "Great, I am so glad I have electricity for another month! And what would it take for this money to come back to me times ten?"

I love asking that question! One time, I paid a lady who did an incredible foot massage for me. I was so grateful for her and I thanked her. As I handed over the money, I playfully said out loud, "What would it take for this to come back to me times 10?" The lady looked at me rather oddly. Later she came up to me and said, "I didn't think I could ask money to come back to me when I paid it out. I thought that would be disrespectful or something. But the way you said it, it was with such gratitude and joy, it was such an invitation. I am going to use that with everything from now on!"

When you are willing to play with money, be grateful for money and be grateful for what you have created and don't judge it, more can show up.

"What if you were willing to be grateful for you, too?"

When you don't acknowledge and have gratitude for the money that comes in and goes out of your life, you are really refusing to acknowledge and have gratitude for you. What if you would start acknowledging yourself for what you have created, what you do have, rather than focus on what you do not have? When you put your attention on what is working in your life, you can create more of it, and it will start showing up in more places. If you put your attention on what you see as lacking, you will only see lack, and the scarcity will grow.

You have to have gratitude for everything you create, the good, the bad and the ugly. That means that you never go to a conclusion, no matter what shows up. How many choices have you judged because you decided you lost money, or you made the wrong choice? How do you know that choice wasn't the exact thing that will allow you to create something even greater in your future? If you judge it, you won't be able to see the gift of your choice, and you will not allow yourself to receive the possibilities that are now available because of it. If you have gratitude, you get to have a totally different reality.

I am grateful for all the people who work with Joy of Business (one of the business's that I own that makes me money and changes the world). We generate business from the joy and curiosity of what is possible to create, not from making the right choice, or avoiding the wrong one.

When someone makes a choice that does not work as well as they would like, we do not give up the joy of creating in business and the gratitude for each other just because it did not show up the way we hoped. We ask, "What's right about this?" and we look at what else is possible that we have not yet considered. The moment you judge, it diminishes possibilities. Gratitude, however, increases them.

If you have gratitude for what people have created, more can show up in your life *and* theirs. If you are joyful with what you are creating and doing, more money will show up.

"Are you grateful when it's too easy?"

A few years ago, I was attending an antiques event run by a friend of mine. I offered to help out by taking money for the items people purchased, writing receipts, general administration. I was doing it because I wished to contribute to my friend and the growth of his business.

After the event, I got an email that said he was paying me a percentage of the sales. I replied, "Thank you, but I don't want the money from that. Seriously, I was happy to contribute."

My friend emailed back, saying, "Be grateful for the money."

I thought, "Well, I am grateful for the money," but I could also see I had an unwillingness to receive it, and I realised that my point of view was that I didn't work hard enough to receive the money. Being there was like being at a party. I was drinking champagne out of a silver goblet, running payments through the credit card machine, and writing out receipts. I was having a fun time. And I get paid for it?

I told Gary Douglas about my shift in perspective and how it seemed to open up so much more in my world, and he replied, "When money comes easily and you are grateful, you are on the way to having a future with more possibilities."

What great future possibilities could you create for your life by allowing money to come easily and joyfully into your life, and by having gratitude for every single cent that shows up?

Chapter 3

How Do You Create a New Financial Reality, Right Away?

What if you had no point of view about money? What if you had no judgements? No financial disasters? No limited financial reality? What if you woke up and started fresh each day? What would you create? What would you choose?

If you really desire to create a financial reality that is different and greater than the one you currently have, you are going to have to look at the choices you are currently making, and if they are not leading you in the direction you truly desire to go - change them! Every choice you make creates something. What do you desire to create with your choices?

It is important to remember that it is not about making a right or wrong choice. It is about making *different* choices.

I talk a lot about business with people all over the world. When it comes to making choices in business, I truly function from, "There is no right or wrong choice, there is just choice." Some of my worst "mistakes" in business were the greatest gifts to me, because they allowed me to see what I could be and do different that would work in the future, that might have taken me a lot longer to become aware of if I had not made that choice. I can see the contribution all my choices are to me creating a greater future because I do not get stuck in the mindset of, "Oh, this choice was wrong and another choice would have been right." What if you never had to get it right, or avoid getting it wrong, ever again?

As my wise friend Gary often asks: "Would you rather be, right, or free? You can't be both!"

If you are willing to be wrong, and give up the need to be right, you can choose anything, and create anything.

"To Struggle, or not to Struggle?"

Years ago I was going to lunch with some friends and I was cranky and grumpy. As we were walking to the restaurant, a friend asked me, "Why are you choosing that?" I said, "I'm not choosing this!" I continued to walk along, all the while thinking, "I am not choosing this! I'm not! Wait, am I really choosing this? Can I change it?" My world felt instantly lighter. By the time we got to the restaurant, I said to my friend, "Wow. I get it. I *am* choosing this. I'm choosing cranky!"

A lot of people don't think that they have the choice to be sad, happy, cranky, relaxed. We are taught to believe that external circumstances create the way we feel about things, but actually, it is just a choice. You have to teach yourself to recognise you have choice, even in situations where you normally assume you have none. What if you would begin to look at all the places where you thought you didn't have a choice and ask "OK, if I were going to flex my choice muscles in this situation, instead of pretending I don't have any, what could I choose right now?"

It is the same with money. If you are currently having upset with money or struggle with money, be aware that it's your choice; you are creating it that way. *And you can choose something else!*

It also doesn't matter whether you have an established business or a salaried job, whether you are a stay at home parent, seeking a job, or on a pension. You don't have to have a lot of (or any) money to start changing your financial reality, and you don't have to have all your ducks in a row, you just have to start. You just have to choose.

In this chapter of the book, we will look more closely at the elements that will help you get out of your own way and allow you more clarity and ease with making different choices with money: having your own back, giving up your stories and reasons for not having money, being honest with yourself and trusting your knowing.

BEING WILLING TO DO WHATEVER IT TAKES

The money tools in this book are fantastic, but to use them effectively to change what is not currently working, you have to have your own back in three ways:

1. You have to be committed to your life.
2. You have to demand of yourself that you will be and do whatever it takes.
3. You have to be willing to choose, lose, create and change anything.

"What if making the commitment to never give up on you was the kindest thing you could do?"

Commitment to your life doesn't mean putting yourself in a straightjacket, or being set on one particular path forever. It means never giving up, never giving in and never quitting. Are you willing to commit to you? Are you willing to never give up on you?

My partner, Brendon and I are both committed to our own lives and to creating a relationship that works for us. We do this by choosing our relationship every day rather than making it a commitment that has to be maintained forever. We make choices to create greater futures for both of us, but we don't ever expect that whatever we choose is set and unchangeable. When we were thinking about buying a house together, I initially resisted as I concluded that we would have to spend the rest of our lives together from necessity. Brendon said, "We can always sell the house," and I said, "Oh, good point!" Owning a house doesn't mean that we have to be together forever; it's still a choice, it's a business deal. Being committed to ourselves is not about committing to never changing our choices. It is making the commitment that we will honour ourselves and each other enough that we can allow ourselves to change our choices when something no longer works.

Committing to you is about being willing to have an adventure of living, to keep choosing what works for you, even if it is uncomfortable, and even if that means making changes and choices that no one else (even your partner, your family or friends) understands. Committing to you can take you beyond your comfort zone, especially as most of us are well trained in giving up what we would truly like to choose in order to fit in with everyone else. You have to be willing to be as different as you actually are, no matter what anyone else thinks, says or does.

"You cannot make a demand of anyone or anything except yourself."

Making the demand of yourself is realising that no matter what, you will have what you desire in your life.

You start creating your life when you finally demand, "No matter what it takes and no matter what it looks like, I'm going to create my life. I am not going to live by anybody else's point of view or reality. I am going to create my own!"

Years ago when I first started travelling for Access classes, I could not always afford accommodation, so I would stay at other people's houses. Once, I was staying at somebody's house, and the house was not very clean. As soon as I stepped out of the shower, I felt like I needed to have another shower. I demanded, "This is not going to work. I have to be able to create more money so I can have a choice of where I wish to stay."

I started staying in hotel rooms with other people and sharing the cost. Then I acknowledged that was not what I desired either. I loved staying on my own. I loved having my own space. There is an energy you create when you make a demand and you do not go to a scarcity reality of lack and doubt.

A lot of times I have demanded for things to show up but I did not really know what that was going to look like. And every time, I made the demand anyway: "no matter what it takes" and "no matter what it looks like." I did not know exactly how I was going to make the money to stay in hotels on my own when I travelled, but I did know I was willing to do whatever it took to create it.

"Be willing to choose, lose, create and change anything."

When you are willing to choose different you are willing to become aware and receive information from the people and things around you, and you have the ability to change in a nanosecond when that will create more for you. It's, "Oh! More information! Okay, let's do this." As you make choices, you might find that things are different from what you first thought. Are you willing to be aware of new information, of the requirement to make a change, or do you try to stick to your first choice, even if it is not working anymore? Or do you make little alterations and then wonder why it isn't changing?

Making little shifts, but essentially doing the same thing (kind of like wearing the same shirt every day and just trying to make it look a bit different, rather than changing the actual shirt) will not get you a different result.

Einstein's definition of insanity was doing the same thing and expecting a different result. You need to change how you are currently functioning to create a different outcome.

We stop ourselves from being willing to do whatever it takes to have a different reality and financial reality when we operate as if there is something fixed and changeless about certain things in our lives. We create something as unchangeable when we think, "This is the way it is."

What have you created as unchangeable? What, for you, is set in stone? What do you see as valuable, permanent, and lasting? Owning a home? Having a long marriage? Owning your own business? Staying in a job? Being in debt?

Are you holding on to any part of your life as if it is a permanent structure? I did this with business. I held on to a business I created way past the time I wished to be involved in it. I tried doing things differently in my business as it started failing, but I wasn't willing to do something totally different and sell my business because I thought I had to do what everyone tells you and keep running a business for as long as possible.

What have you decided you do not have the ability to change? Do you feel choiceless about your financial situation, your lack of money, your debt, or your financial prospects? Have you made a commitment to maintaining the financial structures that you've created in your own universe, rather than doing something completely different? Do you keep trying to change but nothing seems to work? What are you not doing that if you did do it different, would change it all?

I was asking this in a class once and someone said, "Most of the time, I only take action when I am in real pain, and once I am out of the pain, I stop moving forward. Yesterday I realised the amount of money I have is not enough to pay the bills that will be coming in. I suddenly felt the urgency and decided to do something about it. I've always operated like this. I don't take action until I *have* to. It's as if I'm only motivated by pain." If this person was willing to do and be something different with her choice, she could look at the way she functions overall with the "motivation from lack" point of view and ask, "Wait, that is what I have always done. What if I started to function in a completely different way? What would create more for me?" But if she is only willing to ask, "What do I have to do to pay the bills this time?" without looking at the structure she is functioning from, then she will only be doing things a little differently, and won't be able to change her reality with money in the long term.

Another person said, "I find it hard to control my credit card use. It seems like using the card is the only way I can have money. It feels like I have no choice otherwise." If that person went, "I can't use my credit card today, I need to get a loan," that would be doing the same thing, just differently. If they would demand, "I am going to actually create more money now and in the future. I am not living this way anymore. What do I need to put into action right now to change this?" they would be making a different choice that would allow them to create beyond the limited point of view about money they have been stuck in.

You have to be willing to lose all those places, all those structures, all those things you currently believe as permanent and unchangeable. In truth, nothing is unchangeable.

I know that anywhere I am making anything a creation of permanence in my life, I can choose something else. I can say, "That doesn't work for me. I'm not going to choose that anymore."

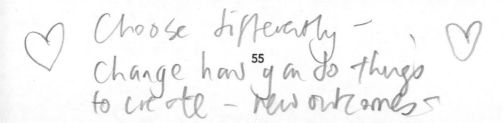

Are you willing to give up the things you decided you have to have, you have to do and you can't or must not lose? What if being willing to lose them was the beginning of total choice? What if you were willing to lose every cent you have? What if you could create far more money than you have ever had before, with total ease?

If you have been trying to change something in your life and it is not changing, take a look at where you might be doing the same thing differently, rather than actually choosing to do something completely different. What would you have to be and do different to truly change your financial reality?

GIVING UP YOUR LOGICAL AND INSANE REASONS FOR NOT HAVING MONEY

You may have noticed that I have used words like "conclusion", "decision", and "judgement" more than a few times by now. Did you know that *conclude* comes from a word that means "to shut up or enclose"? That is exactly what a conclusion does in our lives. It encloses you in a judgement or a decision you have made and it excludes you from receiving any other possibility or seeing any other choice. It is kind of like sticking your foot in a bucket of wet cement and then trying to get somewhere else. You can't do it. You have concluded that's where you are and you cannot change it, unless you let go of that point of view.

We have bought and sold a million stories about money. Lots of those stories we truly believe are right and real, and those are the ones that we love to come back to and re-tell ourselves again and again, instead of simply asking, "Wow, that's an interesting story I am buying into. What if it isn't true? I wonder what else is possible here?"

When my friend was a little kid, his parents used to project onto him that rich people weren't happy. They would take him to see the really nice

what are you doing the same—?

houses in the neighbourhood and he would ask, "Can we please move in here?" and his parents would tell him, "No, we can't afford it. And anyway rich people aren't happy." His response was, "Well, why can't we just try it and see?" He was also told that he shouldn't go eat at the home of the Mexican family in the street because they had less money than his family did. Of course, when that family later bought the vacant lot next door and built apartments on it, my friend realised that his mother had judged them as having less because of where they were from and because they had chickens running around in their backyard and grew their own fruit and vegetables.

Just about everybody has stories like that they can tell, and other insane points of view that they have running in their heads that stop them from having a different financial reality.

Remember the story I told about my Dad? He used to say to us that he would die happy when he knew we (my brother, my step-sisters, my mother and myself) were financially secure. I didn't want my Dad to die, and somewhere in my world I thought if I created debt, he wouldn't leave. That was a pretty insane point of view, and when I realised what I had been doing, I gave it up and changed what I was doing around money, and it started showing up in my life in the most bizarre and unexpected ways.

What financial reality was projected upon you as a child? What crazy points of view have you taken on and bought into about having money, not having money, creating money, losing money and more? What if you could choose to let go of everything you experienced, or believed in the past about money, and did not have to continue to project it into your future anymore?

"Is it time to give up the financial abuse of you?"

The parents of a friend of mine used to tell him, from the time he was just three or four years old, that it was *his* fault that they had no money. He grew up believing he needed to create money for his parents and siblings. Children are aware and they want to contribute. When there are arguments, worries, or energetic undercurrents about money in the house, not to mention blatantly abusive comments, children take them on.

Financial abuse can take different forms but it often results in you feeling as though you do not deserve the most basic things in life. It can show up as living from a sense of scarcity or feeling like you are a financial pain or a burden.

Financial abuse can also take the form of a parent keeping a child dependent and under their control. We were talking about this once in a class, and someone said, "I just realised that my mother wants me to be dependent on her financially so she can feel worthy as a mother. I see how much of my reality around money is based on the desire and my attempt to fulfil her desire to feel useful and vital in that role. And in order for her to feel that, I have to be useless and dependent."

If someone is requiring you to depend on them for money, is that a form of abuse? Yes, it is. Do you have to continue to live by that story now? No, you don't. You have a different choice. You can recognise you received financial abuse in the past, and choose not to have it run your life. You don't have to make it real, you have about a million other choices for your reality with money - at least! And pretty much all of them are much more fun. How about choosing some of those?

"Are you using doubt, fear and guilt to distract you from creating money?"

Do you doubt that you can make money? Do you fear that you will lose it? Do you feel guilty, or blame yourself for debt? Do you get angry about your current financial status? Do you obsess and fixate on problems, rather than look at possibilities when it comes to money? These are all examples of the *distractions* we use to take ourselves out of being present with different choices and possibilities. Every "distractor" we create are the sticky negative emotions we spend our time stuck in, longing to get out of, and firmly convinced we cannot escape. We cement them in with a really good story that explains why you have that going on, so you never have to change it. You will say things like, "I am afraid to because..." or "I doubt I can do that because..." Every "because" is your clever way of buying into your distraction with a great story so that you can give up on you, so that you don't have to change what is going on in that part of your life.

Whenever you get stuck or side-swiped by these distractors, it's actually a choice you are making to judge you rather than to choose a different possibility. What if you began to recognise that the distractors in life are just that, distractions from living your life and creating something different? You can begin to change this by acknowledging the distracting thoughts and emotions when they come up, and when they do, just choose again, choose to ask questions, choose to have gratitude rather than judgement, choose to acknowledge it's not real or true, it's an interesting point of view. You don't have to keep playing them over and over in your head or your life, unless of course you are having a lot more fun being distracted than creating the life and money you desire.

BEING BRUTALLY HONEST WITH YOU (KINDER THAN IT SOUNDS)

You can ask for something different to show up, you can ask to create your own financial reality, you can ask for more money, more currency, more cash flows, more of everything to show up, and yet when you spend so much energy negating yourself, judging yourself and refusing to acknowledge the contribution that you are in the world, you are not being honest with yourself - you are perpetrating some big lies against you to prove that you are not as great as you actually are.

Basically, anywhere you think you are wrong is where you are just refusing to be strong. It's not true that we are wrong or lacking or unable, but it is true that we refuse to be the power and potency we are actually capable of being.

One time I was driving Gary and Dain to a class and I was really angry, but pretending not to be. I was driving pretty unkindly, going over big bumps in the road a bit too fast, and Gary and Dain were hitting their heads on the car ceiling every time I drove over the bumps. I was refusing to talk about it, but then Gary called me early the next morning at 6am and said, "Come over to our hotel room and let's sort this out." I talked to them for ages and ages about why I was angry. I kept saying, "I am judging myself, I am angry at me." But nothing changed or lightened up. No matter how much I said it, it didn't ring true. As we continued to talk and they asked me more questions, I realised that I was, in fact, judging them. I had decided that they were stupid for hiring me. When I was willing to be vulnerable (and yes it was uncomfortable at the time, but I am so glad I did it), I could see what I was doing, and I was able to get out of the anger, and it made it easier for all of us. By judging them as stupid, not only was I not willing to receive the contribution they desired to be to me, I was also not willing to see the contribution that I was to them, I wasn't allowing the business to grow. When I stopped judging them, a lot more became possible.

"Are you willing to have no barriers?"

One of the most prevalent things that occurred after that conversation was how uncomfortable I felt. I said to Gary, "I feel completely disconnected from you and Dain now." Gary asked me, "Have you created your connection with us through judgement?" I realised that I had. He then said, "Well, now you have the chance to create your connection with us based on communion."

Most people will create their connection with someone based on judgement. Judgements create the barriers and the walls that allow us to hide from ourselves and from others.

With communion, it is a space of total non-judgement. And that is completely different. For me it was intensely uncomfortable at first. I felt so vulnerable. All my barriers were down, it was as though they could see right through me.

We are taught to believe that the judgements, barriers and walls we put up will protect us, but in truth, they hide us from ourselves. If you are willing to have no judgement, no barriers, and total vulnerability, you begin to see what is possible for you that you have been refusing to acknowledge.

You've got to be willing to be brutally honest with everything you're creating in your life. It's the only way you can change anything; to have that courage to recognise, "Ok, this isn't working." You have to be willing to have an awareness of what is really going on for you. Creating your own financial reality is about having an awareness of what actually is and then choosing what will create more for you.

What if being brutally honest with yourself was having the vulnerability with you to never lie to yourself ever again?

Being afraid is one of the biggest lies we perpetrate against ourselves. Do you really have fear about money, or losing money or going bankrupt? Do you really have fear at all? Or when some emergency happens do you handle it and then break down later to prove how horrible it was for you?

If you are willing to honestly look at what is going on and to see what is true for you, no matter how intense or challenging it feels, or what you have convinced yourself is really going on, it creates an incredible amount of freedom.

Truly being vulnerable is not about leaving yourself weak, or exposed to attack. To be vulnerable is to be like an open wound and have no barriers to anyone or anything, including you. When you have no barriers or defences, nothing good or bad can stick you. Most of the time we put up barriers thinking we are going to protect ourselves, but what tends to happen is that we trap ourselves behind those walls. When we have those walls, we don't just separate ourselves from other people, we separate ourselves from what is actually true for us. If you truly dropped all your barriers, what beliefs that you currently have about how limited you are would you actually have to acknowledge are not at all true?

Who would you actually be if you never had to defend against or prove anything to anyone ever again? When you judge you and believe you are less than phenomenal, who are you being? Are you being you? Or are you being what other people would like you to be? What if you are not nearly as fucked up as you think you are? What if there is nothing wrong with you that you have to hide, overcome, avoid or defend against? What if you are actually brilliant? Are you willing to see it? Are you willing to acknowledge it and be it in the world?

You being you is one of the most attractive things in the world. And you already recognise it, because the people you are attracted to in life are the people who are being them, who have a vulnerability and a willingness to be present with you. They don't have pretences, barriers or defences. They don't have anything to prove. That is what it is like when you are being you. You don't have to be anything other than you. When you are being you, everyone wants to be around you. And they will be more willing to give you money too, just to be around your energy, just to have some of what you are having. Are you willing to be that irresistible to others?

What if you would demand you be brutally honest with yourself and ask, "Who am I being right now? If I was being me, what would I choose? What would I create?"

"What Would You Truly Like to Have?"

Part of being vulnerable is also about being brutally honest about what you would like to have in your life. If you keep it hidden and secret from yourself, or pretend that you don't desire what you actually want, you have no chance of actually creating and choosing greater and having a life you truly enjoy. You have to be willing to have no secrets from yourself.

Have you ever taken a moment to look at what you would like to create in your life? What if nothing was impossible? What if you could have and be and do and create anything? Have you been willing to be so honest with yourself that you admitted what you would truly like to have in life, even if it makes no sense to anyone else?

What if you wrote out a list of everything you'd like to have in your life? Would you like to have a cleaning lady? A new house? An upgraded kitchen? Is there a trip you would like to take? A business you would like to start? How much money would you like to have in your life?

What is it that you would like for you, and what is it going to take to generate and create that with ease?

Would you be willing to ask for it all, no matter if you believe it's ridiculous, impossible or totally inconceivable? Would you be willing to demand of yourself that you will create it, even if you have no idea how or when it will actualise? Remember: if you don't ask, you can't receive. So why would you not ask for everything you desire and more, and see what can show up, just for fun?

What is it you'd like to request of the universe and demand of yourself? Start writing down what you would like your life and money flows to look like. What is it you would like to create and generate?

TRUSTING THAT YOU KNOW

Was there anyone in your life that empowered you with money and finance? Were you asked what you knew? Were you encouraged to trust yourself and play with money? Probably not. Most of us are not really encouraged to find out who we are and what we are capable of that is unique to us. We are not told to trust ourselves and that we will know what to do. We are taught that we need to look at what everyone else is doing and get on board with that.

When I first travelled, I was only going to go overseas for six months. About three years later I finally returned to Australia. When I did, everyone said to me, "Okay Simone, now you have had your adventure, you can settle down, get a stable job, get married and have a family."

To me, that was the worst thing I could do. My point of view was, "I am just getting started!"

I wasn't willing to follow what everyone else told me I should be. I knew something else was possible, and so I didn't choose what I was told to choose. I trusted that even though I did not have an exact vision of what my life would be, I knew I could create something different. I knew that I loved to travel, I desired to own a business, and I knew I desired to have money, so now it was a matter of choosing it.

"You always knew, even when it didn't work out."

When I met Gary Douglas and I heard him talk about the tools of Access, I knew that it matched what I knew was possible in the world. I trusted myself enough to follow that, no matter what, and I am so glad I did, because it has changed my life, and continues to change it dynamically.

What do you know about money that you have never given yourself the chance to acknowledge, or were made wrong for?

One of our greatest gifts, and the thing we discount the most, is our own awareness of what will and will not work in our lives.

Have you ever known that something was not really going to work out the way you would like, but you did it anyway? Have you ever gone to bed with someone you knew you shouldn't have and woke up the next morning wondering why you made that not-so-great choice? But when it didn't work out, instead of going, "Oh wow, I *knew* that wasn't going to work, how brilliant am I?" you judged yourself and made yourself wrong for it not working out, you think that you created the mess, rather than realising that you knew all along it wasn't going to work, you just did it anyway, thinking maybe you could get away with it! You definitely knew, but you just didn't follow your awareness.

What if you began to acknowledge and trust that knowing, and started to follow your awareness of what would work for you instead of choosing what you know won't really work out? Are you trying to create your life as a success or a glorious failure?

Some of us have spent our whole lives up to now not trusting ourselves. When you have been so committed to delivering what you think other people need and want, you can lose touch with what you actually desire. You can feel blank, or like you don't know. Most likely, you will feel a bit blank for a while as you first start to look at this, because no one has ever really asked you what you actually do desire.

But, please trust that you *do* know. Somewhere, deep down, you know. Maybe you have hidden it away from you for a long time, but you do know.

"If money was not the issue, what would you choose?"

If money was not the issue, what kind of life would you like to have? What would you do each day, what would you like to create in the world? Which of those could you begin to institute right now? Who would you have to talk to? What would you have to do? Where would you have to go? What choices could you make today to start creating your own financial reality?

These are the kinds of questions that I ask myself every day. Each day is new for me. I look at what I desire to create, and I look at what I am creating and what else I can be and do to create more of the future I would like to have.

You can do this too. You can begin to create the reality, the money, the business, the awareness, the consciousness, the joy and the life and living that you truly desire. Trust you. Be willing to recognise that even if it's been 10,000 years since you actually asked for the awareness of what you desire, you do know, and you can create it with more ease than you think!

Part Two

Money Come, Money Come, Money Come!

Chapter 4

Ten Things That Will Make The Money Come (And Come And Come)

By now hopefully you have begun to lift the fog on the places you have been functioning from with money and are starting to look at your financial reality from a place of more space and possibility than when we began.

Having a financial reality that works for you means getting really intimate with what you truly desire to create, not just the amount of money you desire to have in your bank account, but with your life. When you become clearer on the future you desire to create, it's easier for money to come to you. Also, changing your point of view and how you function energetically with money is just as important as the "doing" elements, you need to change all of it to have a different reality with money.

These next 10 elements take a closer look at the pragmatic and hands-on components to changing your financial world. If you do these things, they will work. You do have to do them - you have to choose.

Remember - if you do not make the commitment to you and demand that you will do whatever it takes, no matter what it looks like, it's going to be a lot harder to change things. At the end of the day, what can you possibly have to lose? Your limitations around money? Your angst around money? Your lack of money?

Let's get started. Here are 10 things you can do in your life that will make money come, and come and come:

1. Ask questions that invite money
2. Know exactly how much money you need to live - joyfully
3. Have money
4. Acknowledge you
5. Do what you love and brings you joy
6. Be aware of what you think, say and do
7. Stop being vested in the outcome
8. Give up believing in success, failure, needs & wants
9. Have allowance
10. Be willing to be out of control

I have already introduced a lot of these concepts in Part One of the book so that you become familiar with how it works when it comes to changing debt and the way you function with money. In the following chapters we will get down to the pragmatics and apply these 10 concepts with tools and techniques to really create change in these areas, so that you are free to choose, create and enjoy money, rather than have angst and struggle with money.

Chapter 5

Ask Questions that Invite Money

You may have noticed that throughout the book, I have invited you to ask many questions of yourself about money. It is because questions are the invitation to receive, which allows money to show up. If you do not ask, you cannot receive.

There is a "Golden Key" when it comes to asking questions that you need to be aware of: true question is not about getting an answer, or about right or wrong. It is about opening up to the energy of a *different possibility*.

We have been taught to ask questions from the point of view of looking for the right answer, and we have been taught to say a lot of statements, put a question mark on the end and pretend that we are asking something when in fact we are not. None of that is asking genuine questions. Basically, if you are asking a question and it leads you straight to an answer, a judgement, or a conclusion, or you are using it to try and engineer a particular outcome, rather than from curiosity and the desire to generate greater possibilities for you, it is *not* a question.

For example, here are statements that look like questions, but aren't: "How do I get this to happen my way?" "Why is this happening to me?" "What did I do wrong?" "Why are they so mean?" "Why didn't they offer me a raise yet?" "What the f*&$?" All of these are statements, and already have an underlying assumption, conclusion or judgement, mostly, that you, or something is wrong. Somewhere there is an implied answer, and not a possibility. You could instead ask, "What possibilities are available that I have not yet asked for?" "What did I choose to create with this, and what other choices do I have?" "What's right about me that I am not getting?" "What if someone's choice to be mean had nothing to do with me, what would I choose?" "What would it take for me to be willing to ask for a raise, and what could I create so that I generate more money regardless?" and "What am I aware of that I have been unwilling to acknowledge?"

Another key to asking questions is keeping it simple. Opening a door to a different possibility is as simple as wondering about what other possibilities there might be. If you just walked around today, all day, asking two simple questions, "What else is possible?"® and "How does it get any better than this?"™ with everything that shows up, you would begin to invite a whole new plethora of possibilities and choices you did not have before, when you were not asking anything.

> *"Question goes in partnership with choice, possibility and contribution."*

When you ask a question, you start to become aware of possibilities and different choices you have available. When you make a different choice, you become aware of even more possibilities and choices. When you ask a genuine question, you open the door to the universe being able to contribute to you.

Think of the universe as your best friend going, "Hey, let's play!" It desires you to have exactly what you ask for and will contribute to whatever you are creating in life.

The universe does not have a point of view about what you choose. If your choices demonstrate a preference for struggle, limitations and no money, that is what the universe will give you. If you start to ask for its contribution from a sense of play and curiosity, that is the energy and possibilities and choices it will show you.

Your choices and the possibilities you choose demonstrate to the universe the direction you desire to go. What are your choices demonstrating? What different choices could you begin to make right now? Are you willing to play with the universe 24/7 ?

If you desire to create more awareness of what is possible, ask, "What can I be or do different each day to become more aware of the choices, possibilities and contributions that are available to me in every moment?"

"Start asking for the money, now!"

Most of us have not been taught to ask for money; especially not out loud, and especially not without being extremely uncomfortable or awkward. So you may need to practice. Stand in front of the mirror and ask, "Can I have the money now please?" Say it over and over. Practice as you are driving the car. Keep asking. When you have a client who needs to pay you, or someone owes you money on an invoice, ask, "How would you like to pay for that?" It might be uncomfortable at first, but you have to start asking or you cannot receive!

Imagine if you had total ease with asking for money, from anyone, at any time. How much more freedom would that give you to choose what worked for you? How much more peace? How much *fun* could you have asking for money to show up in all kinds of ways?

"Use questions daily to invite money."

Here is a list of really great questions that you can ask every day to invite more money into your life:

- *What else is possible that I have not yet asked for?*
- *What possibilities are available that I have not yet instituted?*
- *If I was choosing my financial reality, what would I choose?*
- *What would I like my financial reality to be like? What would I have to be or do different to create that?*
- *What can I be or do different today, to generate more money right away?*
- *What can I put my attention on today that will increase my money inflows?*
- *What can I add to my life today, to create more revenue and creation streams right away?*
- *Who or what else could contribute to me having more money in my life?*
- *Where can I use my money so that it makes more money for me?*
- *If money was not the issue, what would I choose?*
- *What action can I do today to change my financial reality?*
- *If I were choosing just for me, just for fun, what would I choose?*
- *Who else? What else? Where else?*
- *And remember… Can I have the money now please?*

Remember that having money in your life is about creating a life and entire financial reality that works for you. Start asking these questions every day and notice what differences begin to show up. Maybe some unexpected possibilities will show up, maybe you will notice that you are less reactive in certain situations than you were previously, or that the people around you start to change. Whatever it might be, take notice and acknowledge it, be grateful for it and do not come to a conclusion around it. Keep asking questions. No matter what shows up, ask for more, ask for greater. What if asking questions became so natural to you that you become an unstoppable, walking, talking invitation for possibilities with money?

Chapter 6

Know Exactly How Much Money You Need to Live - Joyfully!

When people ask me how they can get out of debt and have all the money they desire, my first question is: do you know exactly how much money you need to generate each month for that to occur? Most people tend to create debt because they are not really aware of how much they actually require to live the life they want. I encourage people to ask, "What is required to increase my monthly income? What would it take to have my revenue be greater than my expenses?"

Here's something I strongly recommend that you do: Have a detailed look at how much it costs to run your life. If you have a business, do this for your business too.

If you have a profit and loss statement or some sort of report from your bookkeeper, use that to figure out what it costs you to run your business or your life each month. If you don't have a statement, write down all your living expenses. Write down what you pay for your electricity and all your utilities, how much it costs to run your car, what it costs to run your house, your rent, your mortgage, school fees, everything.

Then, add up all your current debts. If you have around $20,000 or less in debt, divide it by 12 and add that in. If it is over $20,000 of debt, divide it by 24 months or more if you like. Just include that in the list (this is the amount you are asking to pay off your debt each month).

Next, write down what it costs to do the things you do for fun. If you like to get a massage every month or every two weeks, include that. If you get facials and haircuts, write those down. What do you pay for the clothes, shoes, and books you buy? What do you spend when you go out for dinner? Write it all down. If you would like to do more travel, visit family, go on a couple of vacations a year, add that in too. It makes me happy to have a couple of bottles of great wine or champagne in my fridge at all times so I make sure to include that when I am working out my monthly expenses.

Once you have included all the fun things, add it all together. When you have the total, add ten percent of whatever you earn, just for you. This will be for your 10 percent account. In the next chapter, I am going to tell you why creating a 10 percent account is such an amazing and essential tool, but for now, be sure to set aside 10 cents of every dollar that comes in. And then, add another 20 percent, just for the fun of it, because you never know what shows up, and the idea is you are prepared for anything and do not limit your choices.

What is the total amount? This is the actual amount you need to run your life each month. If you are like most people, it is usually quite a bit more than you are currently earning.

The first time I did this, the amount of money I needed to create my life was double the amount that I was actually earning and I immediately went in to overwhelm, thinking, "Oh! I could never earn that much money!" But I didn't stay in that place. I demanded of myself that no matter what it took, I was going to create that amount of money and more, and I asked instead, what would it take to create this *and more*, with total ease? I now earn way more money than that initial shocking amount I came up with. I now do this about every six months. My life changes all the time, so my expenses have changed and I desire to have total awareness of what I am creating so I can demand that more shows up.

76

This exercise is not about trying to cut down your expenses or limit yourself in some way. Most accountants or bookkeepers will look at your information and say, "Your expenses are too high. They are greater than your income. What can we cut out?" That is not my approach. My point of view is: What else can you add to your life? What else can you create? That's why I also recommend you do this exercise every six to 12 months, because as your life changes, your expenses and your desires and your requirements financially will also change.

What if this was the beginning of your ever expanding financial universe? You have to give yourself the gift of awareness of exactly where you are and exactly where you would like to be, or you cannot make the next movement forward, as you will always be unaware about where your finances are.

What if you did this to increase your awareness? What if you did this for the fun of it? What if you did it just to become aware of what you desire more of in life, and to see what else you could create? What if you came out of the trauma and drama of no money and started to create an entirely different reality? This is your life. You are the one who creates it. Are you happy with what you are currently creating or would you like to change it?

Chapter 7

Have Money

In Chapter Two of this book, I talked about being willing to *have* money if you desire to create your financial reality, and what that begins to create in your life when you do.

Allowing yourself to truly have money creates an ongoing sense of abundance and wealth in your life that will contribute to you creating a greater financial future.

I have this strange obsession with water, I like to have a bottle of water on me at all times. I often say I must have died of thirst in a past life, because I noticed that whenever I have water on me, I don't feel thirsty, even if I don't drink any! If I don't have water on me, then I start to feel thirsty. What if it is the same with money? What if having money creates a sense of peace with money that allows you to go beyond any sense of lack?

How do you start having more money in your life and create that sense of wealth and abundance?

Here are three ways you can implement having money in your life. These are simple yet effective tools from Access Consciousness, and some of the first tools I started using to change my own financial reality (and yes, I resisted them first as well and then figured, what was the worst thing that could happen if I gave it a go?). Use them and watch your money expand in your life and grow in your future. I recommend doing all of these and really committing to it for at least six months and see what it changes for you.

TOOL #1 FOR HAVING MONEY: THE 10% ACCOUNT

One of the first important money tools I would like to give you is putting away 10 percent of everything you earn, 10% of every single dollar, euro, pound, or whatever currency you create. You are not setting it aside to pay bills with. You are not saving it for a rainy day. It is not for when you run out of money. It is not to pay a big bill that is upcoming. It is not to help a friend out. It is not for buying Christmas presents. It is for none of those things!

You are putting it away as an honouring of you.

People say, "I've got bills to pay! How can I put away 10% of my income? I have to pay the bills first." But, here's the thing: if you pay your bills first, you will always have more bills. When you pay the bills first, the universe says, "Oh, okay. This person wishes to honour their bills. Let's give them some more bills." If you honour yourself by setting aside 10% first, the universe says, "Oh, they are willing to honour themselves. They are willing to have more," and it responds to that. It gives you more.

Setting aside 10% is gifting to *you*. It's about you being grateful for yourself.

When I first did my 10% account, I was doing it grudgingly because Gary had suggested to do it. The 10% account will not work if you do it from the point of view of, "This book or person said to do it." You have to do it for you. You have to do it to change the energy you have around finances and the energy you have around money. Not just because I said so and you read it here in this book. Start making the demand to create a different reality.

Ask, "What would it take for this to be a choice for me and not a necessity?" What is the worst thing that can happen? You spend it? But you cannot do it from the point of view that you are going to spend it. After around three or four months of starting my 10% account, the energy of money changed for me. I no longer had this panic about money. How many of you have a panic about money, or a stress about money, and that has become more normal to you than not? If you look at the energy of this, it's contractive; it's like throwing the depressing party that money doesn't want to show up to. Money follows *joy*. Joy doesn't follow money.

What I recommend is you start it today. Even if you have a whole pile of bills. Even if you've only got $100 in your wallet and you are thinking that you have to buy the groceries and so on. Start it today. The thing is, this is not logical or linear. You can do the maths around it, but this is not computable. Energetically, the universe starts to contribute to you as well and you start to have money show up in the most random places.

Somebody told me she keeps putting money into her 10% account and then when the bills come in, she uses that money to pay off her bills. She said, "I pay all my bills in full every month, which is great, but I want to change the priority from paying bills to putting that money into my 10% account, and keeping it there, as a way of honouring me." She asked, "How do I stop running out of money between paychecks?"

I said, "My question would be: How many conclusions have you gone to that you will not have the money to pay the bills if you don't use the 10% account?"

The logical point of view might be, "Well, I have to pay the bills, and the only money I have is the money in my 10% account, so I have to use that." I am asking you to *not* function from the logical point of view. This is where choice comes in. I'm inviting you to have the courage to demand, "You know what? I'm not spending my 10% account." And discover what else is possible for you to create.

At one point, the balance due on one of my credit cards was extremely high. I had three times the amount due in my 10% account, so I knew I could pay off the balance on my card if I chose to. I did not do that. Instead I looked at what energy that would create for me if I used the money in my 10% account. I got the sense of that energy, and then I looked at what it would create if I did not do that and instead demanded that I create and generate the money to pay off the credit cards. For me, that second energy of creating more to pay off the cards felt like a lot more fun.

So, that's what I chose.

TOOL #2 FOR HAVING MONEY: CARRY AROUND THE AMOUNT OF CASH YOU THINK A RICH PERSON WOULD CARRY

How different would you feel about your life if you saw a big wad of cash every time you opened your wallet or purse instead of a lot of blank space and some scrunched up receipts? What if you enjoyed having money in there? Carry around the amount of cash that you think a wealthy person would carry.

I travel a lot, so it is really fun for me to have my cash in different currencies. I also have a gold coin in my purse. It makes me happy to have it there. It makes me feel abundant with money. For me, this works. What would work for you? What would be fun for you? What makes you have a sense of wealth?

I like to have at least $1,000 on me at all times. I like to have a bottle of water with me at all times. I like to have a cold bottle of wine in the fridge at home. These things make me happy; they're joyful for me. They provide for me the sense that I'm creating my life. What gives you that sense that you are creating your life that if you actually chose it, would create a different financial reality for you too?

Some people balk at the idea, thinking, "What if I get mugged, or lose my wallet or purse?" I had a young friend who carried about 1800

USD on her at all times and lost her purse. It wasn't very nice for her at the time, but after that, she was much more willing to be aware of her money! If you are worried something like that might occur for you, my question would be, "How much money would you need to carry on you so that you are willing to be aware of it at all times?" When you carry around a large enough amount, you will suddenly become willing to be way more aware of your money; you will become conscious of where it is and what you need to be aware of so that it doesn't get stolen or lost. If you avoid having money on you or in your life because you think you will lose it or it will be stolen from you, you will never allow yourself to have money at all. You have to be willing to have money and you have to be willing to enjoy it without a point of view.

TOOL #3 FOR HAVING MONEY: BUY THINGS OF INTRINSIC VALUE

I have purchased lots of gold and silver with my 10% account and it's fun for me. I have a safe in my house where I keep a lot of my gold and silver. If I ever get the feeling that I don't have money, I will go and look in the safe and realise, "Oh, I do have money." That's the sort of thing the 10% account can do for you.

Buying items of intrinsic value (that means that by the nature of their material they have monetary value) is a way to enjoy having money, and to also have liquid items (liquid means easily sell-able for cash) in your life that will maintain or increase their value over time. Things like gold, silver or platinum can be bought in ounces, kilos or coins. Purchasing antiques or antique jewellery can be a good investment too. They retain their value over time, unlike modern furniture or costume jewellery which may look good, but immediately lose a large proportion of their retail value once purchased. Things like sterling silver flatware are great liquid assets because they are aesthetically beautiful items you can actually use which will contribute to creating a feeling of wealth and luxury in your life. Isn't it much nicer to drink champagne out of beautiful crystal, or a sterling silver goblet rather than plain glass or plastic? I know it is for me!

You don't have to have thousands and thousands of dollars in your 10% account to start buying things of intrinsic value either. You could start with buying a silver teaspoon to stir your coffee with, and add from there. Just make sure, whatever you do or buy, that you follow what is joyful for *you*. Educate yourself about things of value that would be fun for you to have in your life.

I have also bought diamonds and pearls with my 10% account. I have always made sure that there was enough cash money in my 10account for me to continually have that sense of peace and the feeling that I have money.

How much cash would you need to have in your life to have a greater sense of peace and abundance with money? And what else could you add to your life to create a sense of aesthetics, abundance, luxury and wealth that expands every facet of your life and living?

Chapter 8

Acknowledge You

Acknowledging you is something you are going to have to be willing to do if you desire to have your life and your money flows become easier and more joyful. When you do not acknowledge what is actually true for you, you diminish you. If you do not recognise that you have already created something in your life, you will destroy it in order to believe you have not accomplished anything, and you will go back and start all over again. A much easier way to go forward in life is to acknowledge what actually is, to acknowledge what you have accomplished, to open your eyes to your greatness and not dismiss the things that you have created and changed. This is really important, especially as you keep using these tools and everything starts to change for you. You have to acknowledge you, you have to acknowledge what shows up, even if it shows up looking very different to how you thought it would.

There are three ways you can begin acknowledging you more effectively:
1. Acknowledge the *value* of you
2. Acknowledge what is *easy* for you to do and be
3. Acknowledging what you *create*

"Do not wait for others to see your value."

Are you waiting for others to acknowledge you so that you finally know what you have to offer is valuable? What if you were the one who recognises you are valuable, no matter what anyone else thinks? Most people cannot even see you to acknowledge you, because they cannot see or acknowledge themselves! If you are willing to see the greatness of you, if you are willing to acknowledge you, you will be able to see the greatness in others, and you will be able to invite them to see it for themselves, just by being you.

Maybe you think if you can just find the right relationship, receive more accolades in your job, or get your difficult parent to finally acknowledge you, you will finally feel of value. It has not worked yet because, in truth, no one else can really give that to you. If you do not already feel of value in your own life, no amount of people telling you how wonderful you are is going to be able to penetrate your world. You have to see the value of you first, then it becomes easier to perceive and receive acknowledgment from other people. What if you would start every day by asking, "What is great about me that I have never acknowledged?" "What have I been refusing to acknowledge about me that if I acknowledged it would create my life as far more ease filled and joyful?"

You have to know that you are the valuable product in your life - not because other people tell you that you are, because you just know that you are. This might be one of the hardest things to do at first, because you have to give up judging you in order to truly value you. You have to be grateful, and you have to be honest with you, you have to receive your own greatness with no barriers.

You might have to force yourself to see your value at first. Get a notebook and write down what you are grateful for about you - add at least three different things every day. Make the demand to perceive, know be and receive the greatness of you with more ease. Commit to you, and have your own back in this process.

"What is easy for you that you have never acknowledged?"

Everyone has an area in life where you do things with ease, without thinking about it, without judging it as difficult. You just do it. It is super easy. Do you have a judgement of the things you find easy in life, for example driving a car? Or do you just acknowledge that you are a great driver and that you can handle anything and you can just be it and you can choose it?

Everyone has something (and more often than not, quite a few things) that they find really easy to be or do. If you find something like that in your life, you will probably also find that you have no judgement of it and no judgement of you and how you do it. And you probably do not refer to anyone else about how to do it, either. You just do it; you just be it! Now, what if you would take that energy and ask, "What would it take for me to be that energy with money, too?"

Business is one of those things that is easy for me. I truly enjoy it. To me, business is one of the most creative things you can do. I don't judge what occurs in business, I just choose again. Even when a business didn't work out, it never bothered me to the point where I would judge myself about it. I didn't realise that this was such a different point of view until I was talking to a friend about a colleague who was making what I thought was an insane choice with his business, because there was no joy in it for him. My friend said, "Simone, no one does business for the joy of it!" which totally shocked me. I had to acknowledge that I was really different. Until that moment, I thought everybody did business for the joy of it.

Realising that business was easy and fun for me, but not necessarily so for others allowed me to begin to see where I could contribute to other people, inviting them to have joy in their business. I opened the door to creating more in my life - more joy, more ease, and more money! My business, "Joy of Business" was able to be created and contribute to thousands of people all over the world to have another possibility with business. Every day, I have people getting in touch with me who say they are so grateful for the Joy of Business Facilitators, classes and books. That's how potent we all can be in the world, just by being ourselves and being willing to acknowledge and create with our areas of ease.

What do you find easy to do? What do you find easy that you think has no value? We do not often value what is easy for us, because we believe that anything truly worth having, is difficult to obtain. Or we think that it is only easy for us because we believe anyone can do it. Neither of those points of view are true. If it is easy for you, it isn't because everyone else can do it, or because it is not valuable, it is because you are you, and you have a capacity in that area.

Start writing down the things you find easy, and take a good look at them. Get the energy of what it is like to do those things that are easy. Acknowledge how brilliant you are!

Now, what if you would ask that energy to show up in all the places you decided were not so easy? If you acknowledge that energy and ask it to grow in your life, it can and will. If you do not acknowledge it, you cannot choose more of it.

What if it is that simple? The only way to know is if you try it and see. What are you waiting for? What else can you acknowledge about you that you did not think was of value?

"Do you acknowledge your creations, or do you dismiss them?"

I had a friend whose parents said to her all the time, "Money doesn't grow on trees, you know!" They owned an orchard. For them money did grow on trees. But they didn't see it. They could not receive the joy that came from being people in the world whose money actually did grow on trees.

And with the creation of money, how often do you judge or dismiss the amount of money that does and does not show up in your life, rather than picking up every dollar, acknowledging it and asking, "Oh wow this is so cool, how much fun can we have?"

A friend of mine recently won $20,000 by betting $200 on a famous horse race in Australia. I was so excited for him. When I spoke to him about it, the first thing he did was start to look at who he could gift it to and what he could spend it on. I asked him, "What if you just received this awesome creation? What if you could just have the money?" It was not right or wrong that he desired to gift it and spend it. But he had not really stopped to acknowledge himself. Notice the energy and sense of possibility that would be created in life with an acknowledgment like, "I created something really awesome today. What if I truly received this money in my life, and had total gratitude for it, and me? What if I truly enjoyed my creation? How much fun can I have and what else can I now create?"

We do not allow ourselves to truly marvel at our ability to create. What if you could do that with every bit of money that came in - have total gratitude and total acknowledgment of yourself? When you enjoy your ability to create, more will come your way.

How much are you actually creating in your life that you dismiss? What if you could be totally present with everything that occurs and everything that is created in your life and receive it all, with gratitude?

What do you love doing?

- Gardening, vegetables growing
- teaching new skills.
- Being outside
- Walking

Chapter 9

Do What You Love

Throughout my life, I have noticed that there are people who will do things for money, and there are people who will do things in order to create something different in the world.

For example, I know someone who has a lot of creativity and capacity in her universe, but she keeps going, "Well, if I do this, I want x amount of money. This is what I demand." And it's not a small amount. She demands a lot and she has not done anything yet. She will not create anything until someone agrees to pay her a large sum of money, and that person has not yet seen what she can do. I wanted to ask her, "Why don't you just create and see what shows up?" It is not about believing that you cannot make a lot of money or assuming you have to get paid only a little when you start something new. What if you never let anything stop you from doing what you love? What if you just did it anyway, regardless of the money?

Do not create for money; start creating and allow the money to show up. And when it shows up, celebrate. Be grateful.

And do not stop there, keep adding to your life. Include more of what you love doing. And keep inviting the money to come and play!

"What Do You Love Doing?"

A friend of mine who is a beautician asked me about creating more revenue streams. I asked her, "What do you love doing?" She said, "I love driving."

She lives in California and the highways have eight lanes and they're frantically busy, but she loves driving. I started hiring her to pick me up at LA Airport and drive me to Santa Barbara when I was going there. It is really nice to have someone pick you up at the airport after a fourteen-hour flight. She now picks up three other clients as well. She is doing something she loves and she has created another revenue stream. A lot of people would go, "I like driving but how is that going to make me money? I don't want to be a taxi driver!" rather than just looking at what they do love and being willing to create something joyful for them, like my beautician friend did. It is about choice and possibility and the willingness to receive.

You have to start looking at the things you love to do. Get out a notepad and start writing down everything you love doing. It doesn't matter what it is. Cooking, gardening, reading, walking the dog, talking to people. Don't consider if it is something of value out in the world (because as we already know, if it's easy and fun for you, you tend to automatically assume it has no value), just write it down. If it's fun for you, if you love it, then put it down on the list. Keep adding to it over the next days and weeks. Then take a look - are you doing enough of what you love? Remember - money follows joy! Also, start asking, "Which of these could I create revenue streams with right away?" and notice if one, or a few jump out at you. What if those easy and fun things for you were actually what could make you more money than you can imagine? What would you have to do and who would you have to talk to and where would you have to go to start creating that as a reality, right away? And how much fun could you have creating?

"What Else Can You Add?"

One of my new favourite books about creating wealth is James Hester's _The Penny Capitalist_. Hester doesn't say, "Cut down your expenses." He doesn't say, "Stop spending." He asks, "How can you create more money from the money you earn?" Most of the book is about how to make money from the money you have, whether that's five dollars, fifty dollars, five thousand dollars or fifty thousand dollars.

Gary Douglas is brilliant at this. Access Consciousness is a huge, international business, and in his travels around the world, he delights in buying antiques and beautiful jewellery and selling them in his antique shop in Brisbane. It is another revenue stream for him. He makes a profit from it because it's something that's fun for him and he is brilliant at it.

How many revenue streams could you create today? You don't have to be on one track. You can have multiple streams or tracks going. What if you could create as many as you like? What if you could make money from the money you already have? Currently I have several revenue streams. I am the Worldwide Coordinator of Access Consciousness, I have the business, _The Joy of Business_, which has a book in 12 languages, classes, telecalls and private sessions. I also have a stock portfolio that is growing at a rapid speed, and to date my partner and I have an investment property on Noosa River, Australia. For the sheer fun of it, we have also invested in two racehorses with Gai Waterhouse (one of Australia's top racehorse trainers). Basically, there is no limit to the amount of revenue streams you can ask for. What would it take for you to receive them and have fun?

How many times do you refuse the creation of money because you have decided, "It is too small," or, "It is too hard," or "It is off the track I am on"? What if that was irrelevant? If it's fun for you, it's relevant. Joy will get you further in life than you have ever imagined.

If you are looking for more clients in your business, or you are getting bored with your work, ask: What else can I add here? I'm always adding something new that is interesting to me, because most of the time we don't like to do the same thing over and over again. We do not like the repetition. Most of us get bored or overwhelmed when we don't have enough going on. How can you get bored *and* overwhelmed? It may seem strange, but a lot of people I talk to are in exactly that predicament. They feel like they are overwhelmed with everything going on in their lives and they are completely bored with it at the same time. The automatic response that most people do when this happens is they try to downsize or simplify. But has that ever really helped? What if you try something different? If you think you have too many things going on, you are wrong. You can double it. You can triple it. What else can you create?

If you begin to add more to your life, especially if you are creating with the things that you love, both the boredom and the overwhelm begin to melt away, and life becomes more of a joyful adventure of living.

When I first started as Worldwide Coordinator of Access Consciousness, we were in five countries. Eight to ten years later we were in 40 countries, and now we are in 173 countries. There were many times I could have decided it was too much, or that it was overwhelming, but I realised that when I was willing to look at the entirety of the business from a bird's eye view, and ask questions of what else I could add to the business and what else and who else could contribute, I would know what to choose next.

Practice taking that bird's eye view now with a project or part of your life you tend to go into overwhelm with. Take a look and ask, "Could somebody else contribute to this?" "Could somebody else add something to this?" "Could somebody else do this better than me?" These are all questions you can use so that you don't go into overwhelm, and so that you create more clarity.

When you think you have too much going on, ask "What can I add to my life so that I have clarity and ease with all this and more?" Adding to your life will create more of what you desire, eliminating from your life will not.

"Do you create different from other people?"

When I talked about creating new revenue streams in a class once, one of the class participants said, "I get what you're saying, and I'm working on several different revenue streams while I'm writing a book. Yet I keep thinking, 'This new track is taking me away from my book,' or "My book is taking me away from the workshop I want to create.'"

This is a common concern, because in this reality, people project at you that you should finish one thing before you start another. Is that true for you? What works for you? Is it more fun to have lots of different things going on? Try it and see.

I had a previous business partner who always said to me, "Simone you need to finish one thing and then start another one, you are working on too many things at once." And of course I disavowed my knowing and awareness and I thought that he was right, so I would try to do one thing and complete it and then I would start another thing and it was *driving me crazy*. It was really hard to work that way because it's not who I am and it's not how I create.

When I looked at it I realised that I really enjoy working on at least 10 or 20 things at once. It is joyful for me. I love working on them all at different times and having them lightly tap on my awareness asking, "Hey what about me now?" when they require my attention.

If you didn't judge the way you create as wrong, how much more fun could you have with creating even more? What if you can engage with all of your projects? What if you can have multiple revenue streams that you love to create with?

Creating multiple revenue streams is an important concept. If you have trouble receiving this concept, or you think this cannot possibly work for you, please reconsider. This is the way I create. And it is the way I see so many other amazing people create. You have to be willing to live outside of your comfort zone.

What other revenue streams could you create? Who or what could you add to your life that would increase your income? Again, what if creating new revenue streams was not about being linear? Ask questions, and always follow what is lighter and more expansive for you. Follow what you know - because you always know!

Chapter 10

Be Aware of What You Say, Think and Do

Creating a financial reality that is expansive is so much easier when you create your life as an ongoing, open invitation to money. To be this invitation in your own life, you need to stop doing, saying and thinking the things that uninvite money. Start listening to everything that you talk about or the thoughts that come into your head when it comes to money, especially those things that you tend to automatically believe are true and don't normally question - what if they are not actually true at all?

For example, you see a beautiful car but as soon as you wish for it, you decide you could never afford it. You've just uninvited money. You could invite it into your life by asking, "What would it take for that car or that sort of luxury to show up in my life with ease?" that's a question; that's a demand! Saying, "I can't afford it," is a conclusion and a limitation and a dead end where no money and no other possibility can show up. These are the noncognitive and often automatic ways we go about stopping money showing up in our lives with greater ease.

A good friend of mine is a single mother with two children and she does not go to the place of saying, "I can't afford it." She actually makes a demand list of herself. She demands what she would like to create in her life and then she looks at it and asks questions about how she can start to create it.

She wanted to go on a holiday with her children and went to a travel agent. The lady at the travel agent gave her a quote for going on a tour, and my friend said, "Oh I don't want to go on a tour," and the woman said that it would be a lot more expensive to travel without doing it as a tour. Rather than deciding, "That's way more expensive, I should do the tour," my friend asked the agent, "And how much would it be if I travelled with the kids, not doing the tour, *and* travelled in a better class?" She didn't stop herself or stop the possibilities of what she could create. She makes the demand that is what she will create.

You have to be willing to really pay close attention to what you think, believe, say and do in relation to money - because it is exactly what you will create. Another way of looking at it is, you invoke (kind of like a magic spell) your life into existence by your thoughts, words and actions. For example, "I never have money, I never have money, I never have money," is an invocation. You are invoking no money into your life. How often do you think, "I wish I could do this, but I don't have a choice"? "I don't have a choice" is exactly the reality you create every time you say or think it. You will create your world in accordance with that point of view by not choosing anything. Is that brilliant or what? What you think, say and do is very powerful and is creating your life as it is right now. If you want to change what is not working for you, you have to be willing to come off autopilot and be present with what you are creating.

"Wishing versus Creating."

How often have you put things on a wish list, hoping that it will show up, but not taken action to creating it?

I see so many people who do not want to commit to creating a different financial reality, but they still want all the results. They say, "I wish I had a million dollars." They complain or go into the trauma and drama of what they do not have, yet they do not take a single step towards creating it. If you were willing to be totally honest with yourself right now, how familiar is that scenario? What are you wishing for, rather than committing to the creation?

Commitment is the willingness to give your time and energy to something that you believe in. What if you actually believed in creating a million dollars and it was not just on your wish list?

Wishing is basically what you choose when you have already decided you cannot have it. When you wish you had a million dollars, rather than asking questions and taking the steps to create that showing up in your life, you will judge the fact you do not have it; you judge why you do not have it, you judge other people who do have it and you judge that you would never be able to do it. You come up with this list of reasons and justifications of why it cannot be, rather than committing to your life and committing to creating the one million dollars.

There is a brilliant quote from Gary Douglas: "The only reason you choose judgement is so you can justify what you don't have to be committed to." When you are wishing, you are choosing to be committed to the judgement of what you say you desire; you are committing to the judgement of you, rather than committing to your life.

If you were to be brutally honest, how much are you committed to your life right now? 10%? 15%? 20%? The great thing about being committed at a maximum of 20% is that when the million dollars does not show up in your life, it is not your fault, because you were only committed 20% anyway. What if you changed that? Are you willing to commit 100% to your life?

What if today, you started writing down a list of what you desire to create in your life and your financial reality, rather than the wish list that will never actualise?

Take a look at your list: ask yourself, are you willing to commit to the creation of those things? Every morning, ask, "What is it going to take to create this?" and "What do I have to put into action for that to occur?" Then, you have to put some effort into creating it. You have to start choosing, and see what can show up.

> *"Choosing in 10 second increments can change your un-invitations to money into invitations_!"*

What if you lived as though you had a fresh choice every 10 seconds? You know what? You do. You can choose in 10 second increments, knowing that no choice you make is fixed in place. Another way to look at it is: imagine if all your choices expired after 10 seconds. If you wanted to keep going a certain way, all you had to do was choose it again - but you have to keep choosing it, consciously, every 10 seconds, so you better make sure it is something you actually desire to have! You could be married in 10 second increments. You could love your partner for 10 seconds, you could hate them for 10 seconds, you could divorce them for 10 seconds, and then choose them again in the next 10 seconds. You could do this with your money. You could choose no money for 10 seconds, and choose creating money in the next 10. What if choice could truly be that easy?

You choose something and then you have a new awareness and you choose again. Every choice gives you more awareness of what is possible, so for what reason would you not make as many choices as you can? The problem is we get stuck in our choices, particularly when we make choice significant. We make a choice significant when we think there is a right and wrong choice.

I spoke with a woman who wished to move from where she was living, but she was judging herself about where to move. She would not make a choice. She wanted her choice to be the best choice, the right choice, the good choice, the perfect choice, and the correct choice. It was as if she thought she had only one choice, so it had better be perfect. But that is not the way it works. Choice is not binary. Choice has and is infinite possibilities.

When you make a choice, that choice creates a reality and it creates awareness. It does not create a significant, unchangeable solidity in your life. We just think it does. We do that with money in a big way. We decide that we cannot lose the money we have, or the money we are currently making, so we will not make choices that we worry might jeopardise what we have. You have to be willing to lose money - you have to be willing to choose it, change it and create it too - you have to be willing to choose all of it.

To get out of the significance of choosing, you have to practice it. Practice choosing in 10 second increments. Start with little things. When I started playing with this tool, I went, "Ok, I am going to walk over here. Ok, I am choosing to make a cup of tea now. Now what will I choose? Oh, I am going to walk outside. I am going to smell this flower. I am going to sit on the chair. Now I am going to get up and go inside." I made myself keep choosing, and remained fully present with each choice. I enjoyed each choice. I did not make my choice significant, right, wrong or meaningful. I just chose, just for fun. Start practicing choice, and be present, look at what each choice creates in your life. How does your body feel, what occurs for you?

If the choice you make works for you, great! Now keep choosing. And if the choice you made does not work for you, keep choosing.

Every time you choose, what if you could give yourself the gift of knowing that it is not stuck in stone? If you choose something and it has cost you x amount of dollars and it does not work out the way you thought it would, you do not have to waste time judging and reprimanding yourself for your last choice! You just have to choose again. Pick yourself up and choose something else. Look at what it is going to take to create what you desire and keep choosing. Judgement will never create more money flowing into your life. Choice will create more money flows. What choice can you make now?

Choosing every 10 seconds is not about being fickle and changing your mind continually so that you never get anything done. It is about giving you greater and greater awareness of the infinite possibilities you actually have available to you and being able to make choices of any kind with ease and joy. It's about knowing you can choose a choice, and change your choice; you can keep choosing and actually create what you truly desire.

What if you could make life-changing, reality-changing choices, every moment of every day? The choice to never judge yourself again would be a very big choice indeed. Imagine what a difference that would create in your life. It would change everything. Is that something you would be willing to choose sometime this year or next year? What are you waiting for?

Chapter 11
Stop Being Vested in the Outcome

When it comes to making choices in life, how vested are you in the outcome before you even get started? I have some information for you: whatever you decided it must show up as is often a limitation. The universe is capable of delivering far greater. It wants to give you the entire ocean of what is possible, but you are sitting there on the beach looking at only one grain of sand.

If you gave up being vested in how things show up, how could they show up way beyond what you can currently imagine? What if instead of believing you need a particular result in your life, you committed to making choices that totally *expanded* your life and living, no matter what they actually looked like?

> *"What can you do to have more ease with making choices that will expand your future and create more money?"*

When you are faced with making a choice between several options, here are two questions that can assist you:
- If I choose this, what will my life be like in five years?
- If I don't choose this, what will my life be like in five years?

When you ask these questions, do not judge ahead of time what you "think" is the best choice. Just allow yourself to get a sense of the *energy* of what each choice would create. Follow that energetic sense of what is more expansive, even if it does not make logical or cognitive sense to you. What if every choice you make follows that sense of expansion, and it is something that will change other people's realities as well as your own? What if every choice you make to follow that sense of lightness and ease will change your money flows?

My partner and I just did renovations on our house that cost us close to a quarter of a million dollars. We could have looked at that from the negative point of view: "Maybe we can't afford that." "Should we do this, or should we be spending our money on something else?" "The house is fine, we don't really need to do that." But when we looked at what it would create in the future (by asking, "What will our lives be like in five years if we choose this?") it matched the energy of what we desired to create in our life - the elegance, the decadence and the absolute beauty. The aesthetics that Brendon has created is phenomenal. Those renovations have contributed to so many possibilities. For one, Brendon now has the willingness to acknowledge the capacities he has to create something totally different. Nearly every tradesman that comes into our house looks at our bathroom alone and goes, "Wow, I have never seen a bathroom like this!" It's totally unique and different, and it therefore generates a curiosity with what we are creating. For another, our house is now valued at a much higher rate than when we first bought it, which creates the equity for more investment options. How can you spend money today to create more for your future that you have not been willing to acknowledge?

And don't forget that when you have more fun, you make more money.

What if choice was as easy as choosing to cook a meal? What if you could suddenly decide to change an ingredient or add a different spice? What if you could say, "I don't want to cook right now. Let's go out for dinner" rather than thinking, "Oh no, I was really supposed to make this particular recipe at this exact time, and if it doesn't work out that way, that means it's a bad evening and I am a bad person"?

There are areas of our life where we are willing to make different choices quickly and easily, but most of us have made money so solid, real and significant that we think we cannot choose to do something different. The truth is we can. Money is just as easy, quick and changeable as anything else.

"Another tool for choosing - indulge in it!"

Whenever you are considering a choice about something and you are not sure you wish to choose that, what if you would give yourself some time to indulge in it? Indulging in something means, "to yield to, or give oneself over to the pleasure of it." What I am suggesting with this tool is that you indulge in that choice and see what the energy of it is. Let's say you have been told or taught there is a certain structure you need to follow in your business to make it successful. If you are not sure it will work, try it out and see what it creates. Do it for a whole week. Then, for the next week, let that go and choose, "This week I am not going to follow those structures of success. I'm going to follow the energy and make choices based on that." Do it and see what shows up. When I did this, I found that the second approach was much lighter, and it is amazing how many possibilities show up when you are willing to get out of your own way.

For example, I was once told by a business "expert" that I should only send business emails during the week, never over the weekend. So, for one week, I tried to function from the structure I had been told I was supposed to function from. I indulged in that choice. I only sent out emails and made business calls from Monday through Friday. By the weekend I was back to doing what I did before which was following my own awareness and sending emails and making calls when it felt right for me. Even if it meant I was sending an email on Sunday night. I realised that "business hours" didn't mean anything to me. Any hour was a business hour, it is all about the joy for me. My business also expanded more when I did what worked for me, too.

This tool has all kinds of applications. When my partner Brendon and I were first talking about renting a big house, we had not yet lived together and it was a big commitment for both of us. He was saying, "I don't know if I want to do this."

I said, "Well, why don't you indulge in it?" So for three days, he indulged in not moving in with me, and for the next three days he indulged in moving in with me. At the end of that time, he said, "That was easy and obvious, I would much prefer to live with you. It feels way more fun."

When you indulge in something, you have way more awareness of the energy that would be created or generated by choosing it. You become aware of what it would create. So indulge in possibilities. Indulge in the concepts of success of this reality, the structure of success, and then do not indulge in that. Indulge in following the energy and going against the rules of this reality. Which one is lighter for you?

If you had no rules and regulations and no reference points, what would you create? What if there was not an ultimate goal or ideal outcome, just infinite and unlimited creation? What would the adventure of making money be for you today? What would be the adventure of living today? In adventure, there are no rules and regulations there are infinite possibilities from which you can choose!

What if you simply chose something different, just because it was fun for you?

Chapter 12

Give Up Believing in Success, Failure, Need's & Wants

Many of us believe that *success* is defined by getting a whole lot of things right in life. But success is not about how we get it right. I was once conducting a series of teleclasses and someone said to me, "I've really enjoyed your calls." I instantly focused on getting it right and thought, "Shit! I've got another three calls to do. What if they are really bad?" That's insane! These points of view can come up so quickly. Where did we decide we had to get it right? There is no *right*. There is no *wrong*. Success is also not about the amount of money in our bank account. Success is creating what we desire in the world, whether that be money, change, awareness or consciousness. How many times have you received exactly what you wanted or aimed for? Even if it didn't always work out in your best interest, anything you have really desired, you have created.

For me, I desired to change the way people see the world. If I have succeeded in changing one person's point of view - I am a success. From that point of view, I am a success more than a thousand times over. Where are you a success already that you have not acknowledged? You have been spending your whole life thinking you need to be successful to change things. You already are successful, and if you want to change things in your life too, you can just change them.

"Falling and Failing"

Many years ago, I had a huge accident on a horse. After that, whenever I rode a horse, I rode with the point of view, "I wonder how I'm going to fall off?" or, "I wonder when I am going to fall off?" It was all about falling. When I go snow skiing, it's totally different. I never have the point of view that I'm going to fall. I don't care if I fall. If I fall when I am skiing, because I ski really fast, usually it's a huge tumble, with skis and legs and everything everywhere. And it's fine for me.

I ski for the fun of it. I ski for the joy of it. I'm always asking Questions "What else can I do? What jump can I go over? How quickly can I ski through those trees?" It's an adventure. It was not at all like that when I was riding a horse. I know people who have the completely opposite point of view - they love riding horses and don't care if they fall off, but they freak out about skiing. The only thing that creates the difference between what is fun, what is falling and what is failing, is our point of view and nothing more. Failure is a total lie. Judgement will always stop you from creating more.

What have you decided that you have to get right? Have you decided that your business has to be right? Or that you have to make the right decision? Or that you have to avoid wrong decisions, or avoid falling and failing? What if you knew that choice creates awareness? Have you spent a bunch of money on something that did not work? Okay, choice creates awareness. So, what do you want to choose now? A choice that did not work out like you planned is not a failure, or wrongness. It is just different from what you thought.

"What if it's time to be as different as you truly are?"

What if you are not a failure or wrong, just different? What if you are different from what you thought you were, and you can start to choose what will work for *you* and no-one else? Are you actually going to fail? Or are you going to create something that is totally different from what you've created before?

Here's an exercise you can do to acknowledge your difference and give up the failure mindset:

1. Write down what you believe are your failures in life. Did you fail at a business? Did you make a choice that lost money? Did you have a terrible relationship break up? Did you fail math at school? Once you have written them down, take a look, and for each one ask, "If I didn't judge this as a failure, what contribution can I receive from this?" and "What awareness did this create in my life that I would not have otherwise?" Write down what pops into your head. Get out of the judgement of your choice and ask to become aware of the contribution, the change, the awareness that it created for you.

2. Write down what you believe are your "personal wrongnesses." What do you judge yourself for being and doing? Procrastinating? Being messy? Always having to get it perfect? Have a look at the list of things you judge yourself for being wrong for. Ask, "If I took away my judgement of wrongness around this, what strongness would this actually be?" You may think there is nothing strong about procrastinating, but I find that most people who procrastinate either have a great awareness of the timing of things that they have not acknowledged, or they are actually capable of creating far more than they thought and do not have enough going on in their lives. What they were judging - the procrastination - is actually a strongness and a capacity that they haven't acknowledged or fully taken advantage of yet. What if that were true for all your "wrongnesses"? How many strongnesses of you can you begin to uncover with this exercise? You might soon discover you are not wrong.

"I don't need or want money
- and neither do you!"

Money doesn't come to those who believe they lack. The truth is, you do not lack of anything. If you are alive, you are not lacking. If you wake up in the morning, you have everything you need to create everything you desire. Needs and wants are about living in the lie that you lack.

Did you know that the original meaning of "want" in any dictionary prior to 1946 has 27 definitions that mean "to lack" and only *one* that means, "to desire"? Every time you say, "I want", you are actually saying, "I lack"!

Will you do something for me right now?

Say out loud 10 times in a row: "I want money." Do it now. What is the energy that comes up when you say it? Is it light, fun, or heavy and weighing you down?

Now, say this 10 times in a row, out loud: "I need money." Do you get a similar result?

Finally, try saying, "I *don't* want money," out loud, at least 10 times and notice... Does it feel any different at all? Did you start to lighten up? Did you perhaps start to relax, smile or even giggle a little?

That lightness that you feel is the acknowledgment of what is true for you. Because, in truth, you don't lack anything.

"Necessity and Choice"

Last year, I came home after being on tour for what felt like five thousand years. After being used to living in hotel rooms that were always serviced and then walking into our home that had the dust and grime from renovations, I got cranky that things were not "right" about the house. I complained, "I wish just once I could walk into this house and everything was in place and everything was spotless." Brendon asked me, "What are you doing? What is behind all of this?" and I said, "I don't want to play house anymore. I don't want to do this anymore. I don't want to come home and the laundry is full, filled with washing and then there's dishes to do!" I actually love being at home, but the energy I created with the upset was not really creative, it was contractive. I started concluding from an anger, a frustration, that I have to deal with this, that it is a necessity and a problem, that there is no way out. I wasn't looking at what I would like to create. I was thinking that I didn't have a choice about the state of the house.

Brendon said, "We are earning enough money, we could hire someone. I know we have a cleaner once a week, and we could hire someone else to come in a couple of hours and do this," and he was right. Once I took a moment to breathe and look at it, I asked, "You know what? I would like my house to be like this, I would like to choose to do this," everything became a whole lot easier. Instead of concluding that I had to deal with it in a certain way (like having to clean up the house myself) a necessity, I could see the choices that I had, I could let it be dirty, I could clean it myself, or I could choose to hire someone to clean it for me and I am sure there are even more choices available that I had not considered. Now we have a property manager that handles everything for us with all of our properties. Easy.

What if everything is actually a choice? Even getting up in the morning is a choice. You don't have to do it. You think you do, but in truth, it's a choice you make. What if it was a choice you can make, joyfully? You choose to live with your kids and your husband. You choose to keep going to your job each day. What would you like to create?

Just like success and failure are a lie, so are needs and wants. For you, it's really just about choice, awareness and more choice. And that is how you create money - by choosing, choosing and choosing again. If you choose not to judge you or anything in your life, you can no longer believe you are a failure, or that you lack. When you choose to never judge you, you begin to see that the right and wrong, the good and bad, and all of that polarity is neither real or true and that all you have to do is choose more or less of what you desire. It is totally up to you.

Chapter 13

Have and Be Allowance

Allowance is where you are the rock in the stream. All the points of view in this world about money wash right over you, but they do not carry you away with them. You do not become the effect of all around you.

How often do you take on someone's judgement of you and allow it take you down a black hole, where you feel bad, wrong, upset or hurt? Allowance gives you the ability to not take on other people's judgements, or to judge yourself, no matter what occurs.

At one time, there were some people in Australia I'd known for several years who were judging me nonstop. They were saying things about me that were very unkind and mean. I was upset and I spoke to a friend about it.

The friend said to me, "You must be one powerful mo-fo to have that occurring."

I said, "Oh!"

My friend said, "Have a look at *their* lives, and then have a look at *your* life."

I looked at how much my life had grown in the years I had known them and how small their lives had become. I realized they were not actually judging *me*. They were judging what *they* hadn't been willing to create. I now recognise that when someone is judging me, it is usually not about *me*; it is about *them*. What if you were willing to receive the judgements that others have of you? What if you were willing to receive it all?

Use this as a tool! If you find yourself judging someone, ask yourself what judgement you have of *you* in regards to this person. See if it starts to lighten up. Judgement is not real and allowance creates possibilities.

It is also important to recognise that allowance is not acceptance. It is not trying to make believe everything is okay. I chose not to continue having those people as my close friends. I did not decide that I had to accept what they were doing and put up with it, I still included them in my life, and I was in allowance that they chose to judge me. I did not need them to change to have a sense of freedom and not be at the effect of their judgement.

"Are you willing to be in allowance of you?"

Do you find that you are far more willing to give up your judgements of others than you are of yourself? This is because you are not truly a judgemental person. You do not actually judge other people. You will however, judge yourself 24/7 for all eternity, whilst believing you really are judgemental of others. What if you gave up judging anything about yourself? Most of the judgements we have about ourselves, 99% of them are ones we have picked up from the people around us. We have seen them judge themselves and each other, we have learned to take that on and bought into all of it. Interesting choice, huh?

Would you be willing to start being much kinder to you? You can recognise, "Right now I am choosing to judge me. I am going to enjoy that for a minute, and then I am going to choose to stop judging me." You can choose to judge you, and you can choose to stop judging you. Do not judge your judgement! You can believe you are really messed up for a minute, 20 minutes or a day, or 10 years if you really want to. Then you could ask a question like, "What's right about me that I am not getting?"

Allowance for you means never judging you - even if you are judging. Even if you have messed up, or done something you know was not your brightest choice. What if none of it is wrong? What if nothing you have ever been or done was wrong? And what if nothing about you is wrong? What gift in your life would having total allowance for you actually be? Imagine never judging your choices with money ever again. You would not have to think about avoiding making mistakes in the future, you would be free to create anything and everything you desire, you would be free to change and choose. But don't choose that, it would be way too much fun!

"Don't try to change people."

I am often asked some version of the following question: "How can I convince my partner to have more positive attitudes about money?" and I will give this response: "It's not for you to convince your partner to have more positive attitudes about money. You have to be willing for him or her to choose anything. You have to be in total allowance of your partner's choices to either have money or not have money."

If *you* are willing to have positive attitudes towards money, if *you* are willing to have the happiness of life and living and money flows for you, you might be surprised to see what shows up for your partner.

You also have to be willing to be you. Have you been holding yourself back because of your partner, your family or the people around you? What if you now chose for you?

There was a time when my partner was going through some difficult stuff. He was lying on the couch for days on end, sad and depressed. I did not try to fix him or change anything. I just checked in with him and kept going about my life. Finally, after several days, he said, "Will you stop being so happy!" It made us both laugh because it gave him the energy of what he was choosing and he saw how much energy he was putting into being sad and depressed.

You being you and choosing what you choose, no matter what it takes, no matter what it looks like, will invite others to a different possibility. Please do not try to tell your partner what to do. It never works. Do you like being told what to do or that you have to change your attitude, your outlook or something you are doing? It is one of the worst things you can do to someone. They will end up resisting you and hating you for it. Let other people choose what they choose, and keep choosing what you choose.

Chapter 14

Be Willing To Be Out Of Control

Sometimes life can seem chaotic. So many things are going on. There is so much to do. We often mistakenly come to the conclusion that if we were just in control of everything, it would get better. That if everyone would do what we said, things would be easier. You know you cannot control anyone else, right? Would you be willing to give up being the control freak of magnitude you are?

Have you noticed that the more you try and control things, the harder and more stressful it gets? How small do you have to create all the components of your life in order to control them easily? How much have you made the money in your life small enough for you to control? What's the biggest amount of money you could handle before you would have to let other people help you manage it? Whatever that amount is, that is the most you will ever let yourself have in life. Do you think multi-millionaires control everything with their money? No! They have bookkeepers, accountants, financial advisors and all kinds of people handling their money.

People who are great with money know that they do not have to control every detail, they can hire people who are better than they are at those kind of things. But they *are* willing to be aware of their money. They are willing to be aware of things when they are working, or when they are not working, and to ask questions when something does not feel right. What if being *out* of control would open you up to have way more going on, and with a lot more ease than you ever imagined? What if not having to define, confine, delineate, conform, or create structure would set you free and allow you to have a much bigger and way more joyful life?

There was a time when it felt like I was single handedly managing so many things. I told Gary that I felt totally overwhelmed.

Gary said, "Let's talk about the difference between *overwhelmed* and *bogged down*. *Overwhelmed* is where you think you cannot handle it. *Bogged down* is getting caught up in the smaller details of all the different projects and all the things that need to be done."

I said, "That's what's happening. I'm totally bogged down." Instead of letting go of the reins and allowing the horses to go in different directions, I was creating control so that "all roads lead to Simone."

Gary and I talked about who could take some things off my plate, and even though I saw that I was mired in the details, I was reluctant to let go of things and let others do them. I did not want any mistakes made with the business of Access. Gary reminded me that mistakes are part of creation too. He said, "There is no wrongness. You have to hire great people to work with you *and* you have to be willing for them to mess up. You have to be willing for them to make a mistake, because when they make a mistake, they will create something greater."

I finally got that I needed to let go of all the small jobs I had been holding on to. When I got someone else to do the jobs and I let go, it created so much more space for me. I was able to create even more in my life, with my businesses, with Access, with so much more ease. This meant that my money and income could increase more dynamically too.

What if you could create your life, business and different revenue streams by expanding your awareness and *letting go* of what you have been trying to control?

"What if you could create brilliantly from the chaos?"

What if you created amazing things from chaos? I used to judge myself for being a very chaotic creator. I once had a business with a partner who was super organised. He had to-do lists and ticked them off every day. I couldn't do that. I would make a call, then I would look at some clients that needed sorting out, work on next year's range and the list would go on. I was all over the place (according to him). When he was going to leave the business, I had to look at if I would sell it or take over the running of it myself. He said to me, "Simone you are too disorganised to run this business on your own!" I thought he knew more about the business than I did. But when I looked at all the things I had done in the business, I actually knew a lot more than he did, it was just his judgement that I did not know what I was doing because my way of doing business was more like chaos, while his was more order.

I see people when they feel like they have a million things to do, they will push things away and they will destroy future possibilities rather than ask, "There's a lot of projects going on right now, what questions do I need to ask to create all of this with ease? Who or what else can I add to my business and life? What would it take for this to be easy, and what requires my attention today?" You don't have to work on everything every single day. Each day is different, each day is an adventure. Each day you need to start functioning from not judging what you are creating or not creating.

When you create from chaos, anything is possible.

For the next week, try letting go of the reins of everything you have been holding onto so tightly. Let go of the projects, family, friends, money you have been trying to control and see if something new can show up. Rather than trying to manage every detail or deal with everything each

119

day, ask: "What do I need to be aware of today?" Ask what requires your attention today, and deal with that. If you wake up in the morning and ask, "What's next?" "What or who requires me now, and what do I need to work on, who do I need to call?" you can put your attention on things and then move to something else and then something else again. What if functioning that way was not wrong? What if you were not being "distracted," or you were not procrastinating? What if that is the way you create?

You will be amazed at what you can create when you allow yourself to have the joy of creating from chaos. This applies to every aspect of your life: relationships, business, family, money flows, your body. Remember, you are not alone in the universe, the universe will contribute to you creating everything you desire, so ask for more.

What have you not been willing to let go of, or give up control of, that if you let go and gave up control of it, could create more space for you?

Chapter 15

A Note About Cash-flow

I once met up with a very successful businessman in South Africa. He was an orphan. At 15 years of age he was kicked out of the orphanage (because after that age you had to look after yourself) so he left with his backpack, looked at what he wanted to create with his life and made the demand of himself to create it. He educated himself and became a lawyer. He has created huge businesses in South Africa - big resorts, an IT company, and more.

I sat down to have a chat with him because I was really interested in the way he created. There seemed to be a huge generosity of spirit in his approach to creating his business and life. One thing he said to me was, "There are three things in life you have to remember - gratitude, belief and trust. And then there's cash-flow." I laughed, knowing he was correct.

He continued, "If you don't have cash flow, you limit yourself. You have to keep looking at moving forward and not holding yourself back, and be aware of your cash flow, too."

Look at the cash flow you currently have or don't have. What would it take to have continuous cash flow in your life? If you have cash flow, it creates more ease and more space for possibilities, it eliminates the places where you go to, "I don't have," or, "I am without." What if you did not have to put everything in one basket when it comes to money? What if there are many possibilities (revenue streams) for money you can choose?

And what if creating cash flow is really just about playing with possibilities and being totally aware of your financial reality?

How many revenue streams can you create? What brings you joy that you could make money from? What are you curious about?

I am incredibly busy with what I choose to do with work and yet I have other revenue and creation streams as well, and keep asking for more to show up each day. Are you interested in antiques, currencies, the stock exchange, buying and selling things on E-bay? What is it for you that can create more cash flow in your life that you have not been willing to acknowledge?

What else exists out there in the world with regards to money that would be fun for you to discover? Start to educate yourself about money. Who are the faces and symbols on your cash currency? Do you know what the largest dollar value bill is in your country, or other countries? What colour is each note, not just in your currency but other currencies as well? Become familiar with money, do not avoid it, admire it, play with it, acknowledge it.

When I became willing to educate myself about money and the innumerable ways it could contribute to my life, I began to be willing to have money. When I allowed myself to have money, I became willing to play with money. Not being willing to educate myself about money created debt. Now that I am willing to educate myself with money, have money and play with money, it creates more. And not from the significance of it all, but truly from the *joy* of it, and the choice of it.

What if now, just for this 10 seconds, no matter what was going on around you, you chose to play? What if you chose to live your life as the celebration it truly can be, and invited money to come along to the party called your life? What if you chose to be happy, to be grateful, to keep choosing, no matter what?

What if creating your financial reality was truly an ongoing exploration of the infinite possibilities for creating your life joyfully, including your revenue streams, and cash flows? What else is possible that you have not yet considered?

Please use this book and its tools as you continue to change your financial reality. It takes courage to keep choosing something greater, something different, and it is not comfortable all of the time. If you are reading this book, if you are alive on this planet, right now, you have the courage, and you have the capacity. All you have to do now, is choose.

Part Three

SUMMARY AND TOOLS

SUMMARY OF CHAPTERS, QUESTIONS AND TOOLS

This chapter contains a summarised reference of the main points, questions and tools of the book. It is one thing to read how someone else changed their life financially, in fact I get it can be frustrating. The unique aspect of this book is that I used the Access Consciousness tools to change my financial reality, and you can too. You do, however, have to keep choosing, no matter how uncomfortable it gets. If you will use these tools every day you will change your financial reality forever. Let the adventures begin.

PART ONE: NEW FINANCIAL REALITY 101
Chapter 1: What Makes Money?

MONEY NEVER SHOWS UP HOW YOU THINK IT WILL

Money is not linear

Money does not show up in your life in a linear way – it can show up in all kinds of ways, from all kinds of places. If you want to make more money in your life, you have to be open to all of the magical and miraculous ways – even if it's totally different from anything you have considered. What if you could have unlimited revenue streams? What if you can create money in ways no one else can? What if you had no point of view about money?

> **QUESTIONS**
>
> * What are the unlimited ways money can show up for me now?
> * Am I willing to give up having to compute, define or calculate how money will show up and allow it to come into my life in random, magical and miraculous ways?

Don't figure out HOW money has to show up

The universe manifests, you actualise. Manifesting is "how" things show up, and it is not your job to figure out how. Actualising is asking for something to show up, letting the Universe do the manifesting, and be willing to receive it, however it shows up.

QUESTIONS

- What would it take for this to show up?
- What would it take to actualise this in my life right away?

Be Patient

The universe has an infinite capacity to manifest, and it usually has a much grander and magical way of doing it than you can predict. Sometimes the universe has to move things around in order to create what you desire.

Do not judge you, be patient and do not limit the future possibilities.

Money isn't just cash

There are so many ways that money and cash flows can come into your life, but if you are not willing to acknowledge them, if you think they have to look a certain way, you are going to think you are not changing things, when, in fact, you are.

Start acknowledging the different ways money shows up in your life. When your friend buys you a coffee, or someone gifts you something. That's money. That's receiving.

QUESTIONS

- Where else am I receiving money that I have not acknowledged?
- Where else can I receive money that I have never acknowledged?

Simone Milasas

ASK AND YOU SHALL RECEIVE

Money does not judge

Money shows up to people who are willing to ask and are willing to receive it.

Receiving is simply being willing to have infinite possibilities for something coming into your life, without a point of view about what, where, when, how or why it shows up. In other words, when you lose your judgments of money, and of you in relation to money, you can receive more.

What if you did not need a reason to ask for money?

What if you could have it just because it was fun?

What if you could just ask for it to show up?

MONEY FOLLOWS JOY, NOT THE OTHER WAY AROUND

If your life was a party, would money want to come?

If you looked at your current life as a party, what kind of invitation would it be to money?

What if you started living your life as the celebration it can be, today?

What if you did not wait for the money to show up?

What brings you joy?

The energy you create when you are having fun, when you are totally, happily engaged in something you love, is generative. It does not matter how you create that energy.

> **QUESTIONS**
>
> - What do I love to do?
> - What brings me joy?

Getting Out of Debt *Joyfully*

Your life is your business, your business is your life!

If you are alive, you have a business – it's called the business of living!

What energy are you running your life with? Are you having any fun?

> **TOOL: DO SOMETHING YOU ENJOY EVERY SINGLE DAY**
>
> ▸ Start doing the things you enjoy for one full hour a day and one full day a week.

STOP MAKING MONEY SIGNIFICANT

When you make something significant, you cannot change it

Whatever you make significant, you make greater than you. Start recognising all the places you have made money significant, and be willing to get out of that point of view and create a different reality for yourself.

> **QUESTIONS**
>
> • How significant am I making money in my life right now?
> • If money were not significant, what would I choose?

Chapter 2: What changes debt?

YOUR POINT OF VIEW CREATES YOUR (FINANCIAL) REALITY

What is your point of view about debt?

If you want to change debt, start by changing your point of view. The point of view you have had about money up until now has created your current money situation.

Instead of judging the debt you have created, empower yourself by asking questions so that you can change things.

QUESTIONS

- What else is possible?®
- What can I do and be to change this?

Have you decided that the solid, heavy stuff in life is real?

What have you decided is real and not real for you? Why have you decided it's real? Because that was your experience in the past? Because it "feels" real: heavy, solid, substantial or immovable? Would something that is true for you really feel like a tonne of bricks, or would it make you feel lighter and happier?

TOOL: "INTERESTING POINT OF VIEW I HAVE THAT POINT OF VIEW"

For the next three days, for every thought feeling and emotion that comes up (not just about money, but about everything) what if you would say to yourself, "Interesting point of view I have that point of view" Say it a few times until it lifts.

TOOL: WHAT FEELS LIGHT IS TRUE FOR YOU AND WHAT FEELS HEAVY IS A LIE

When something is true for us, and we acknowledge it, it creates a sense of lightness and expansiveness in our world. When something isn't true, like a judgement or a conclusion we have come to about something, it is heavy, and it feels contracted or solid.

GIVING UP COMFORT WITH DEBT

What do you love about being in debt and having no money?

If you are willing to ask some questions, you can acknowledge what is keeping you stuck. If you do not acknowledge it, you cannot change it.

QUESTIONS

* What do I love about being in debt?
* What do I love about having no money?
* What do I love to hate about having no money?
* What do I hate to love about having no money?
* What choice can I make today that can create more now and in the future?

BE WILLING TO HAVE MONEY

There is a difference between having, spending, and saving money.

Most people only want money so they can spend it. Having money is different. Having money is about letting money contribute to your life growing.

Saving money is about putting it away for a rainy day. Saving money and having money are different.

Are you someone who asks, "How can I save money?" Is there a generative energy in that question? Does it seem to expand your choices, or limit them? Is there somewhere you are trying to save money? Try asking: "If I spent this money I'm trying to save, would it create more for today and the future?"

- What are the infinite ways I can generate more money?
- What energy do I need to be to create it with ease?

STOP AVOIDING AND REFUSING MONEY

Are you living in a "No-Choice Universe?"

Is there anywhere in your life you refuse or avoid looking at your money situation? Do you have really good reasons to avoid doing simple and easy things to create more money? When you avoid something, refuse or are unwilling to have something, it does not allow you to have more choices or create more. You have to be willing to look at where you are creating a no-choice universe, and be willing to change it.

What's the worst that could happen if you did not avoid money?

What have you decided is the worst thing that could happen if you didn't avoid money or avoid your debt? What could change if you were willing to have total awareness of your financial reality? Do you avoid doing new things that could make you money?

- If I did not avoid this, what could I change?
- What easy ways to make money do I have that I have been avoiding?

GRATITUDE

Be grateful for the money!

When you receive money, notice your instantaneous point of view. Are you grateful for every dollar, every cent, that comes into your life? Or do you tend to think, "That's not much," "It will cover this bill," "I wish I had more"?

> ### TOOL: PRACTICE HAVING GRATITUDE FOR WHEN THE MONEY COMES IN AND GOES OUT
>
> ▸ Practice saying: "Thank you, I am so glad this showed up! Can I have more please?"
> ▸ When you pay a bill, be grateful that you paid it, and ask: "What would it take for this money to come back to me times ten?"

Are you willing to be grateful for you, too?

You have to have gratitude for everything you create - good, bad and ugly. If you judge it, you will not be able to see the gift of your choice, and you will not allow yourself to receive the possibilities that are now available because of it. If you have gratitude, you get to have a totally different reality. Instead of judging you, or anything that shows up in your life, seek the gift in it that you can be grateful for.

> ### QUESTIONS
>
> • What's right about this?
> • What's right about me I am not getting?

Are you grateful when it's too easy?

Do you dismiss things that show up in your life when it comes too easily? Would you be willing to change that? "When money comes easily and you are grateful, you are on the way to having a future with more possibilities." – Gary Douglas.

> **QUESTIONS**
>
> * What will it take to have gratitude for every cent that shows up?
> * What gratitude can I be that would allow money to come easily and joyfully into my life?

Chapter 3: How do you create a new financial reality, right away?

To Struggle, or not to Struggle?

A lot of people do not think that they have the choice to be sad, happy, cranky, relaxed. External circumstances do not create the way we feel about things. Money does not create the way we feel about things. It is actually just a choice you can make.

> **QUESTIONS**
>
> * Am I pretending I don't have choice here?
> * What choices do I actually have?

BEING WILLING TO DO WHATEVER IT TAKES

Making the commitment to never give up on you.

Being committed to you is being willing to have an adventure of living and choose what works for you, even if it's uncomfortable, or even if it involves making changes that no one else understands.

You cannot make a demand of anyone or anything except yourself.

You start creating your life when you finally demand, "No matter what it takes and no matter what it looks like, I'm going to create my life. I am not going to live by anybody else's point of view or reality. I am going to create my own!"

> * Am I willing to demand of myself to create what I desire in my life, no matter what?

Be willing to choose, lose, create and change anything.

Einstein's definition of insanity was doing the same thing and expecting a different result. You need to change how you are currently functioning to create a different outcome.

If you have been trying to change something in your life and it is not changing, take a look at where you might be doing the same thing *differently*, rather than actually choosing to do something *completely different*.

> * What have I decided is unchangeable?
> * What have I been unwilling to lose?
> * What more could I choose if I was willing to lose these things?
> * What can I be and do different to change this?

GIVING UP YOUR LOGICAL AND INSANE REASONS FOR NOT HAVING MONEY

Is it time to give up the financial abuse of you?

Financial abuse can take a different form but often result in you feeling as though you do not deserve the most basic things in life. What if you did not have to live by that anymore?

> ### QUESTIONS
>
> * What stories am I telling myself about money? What if they are not true?
> * Am I allowing financial abuse of that past to run my future?
> * What different choice do I have here?

Are you using doubt, fear and guilt to distract you from creating money?

Any time you doubt, have fear, guilt or blame around money, or you obsess, fixate or get angry about your financial situation, you are distracting yourself from being present with different choices, different possibilities.

> ### TOOL: ELIMINATE THIS WORD FROM YOUR VOCABULARY
>
> ▸ Eliminate the word "because" from your vocabulary. Every "because" is your clever way of buying into your distraction with a great story so you can give up on you. When you catch yourself saying it, ask, "Oh, that's a great story. What else is possible if I don't use this story to stop me?"

> ### QUESTIONS
>
> * What distractions am I using to stop myself from creating money?
> * What else is possible that I have not yet considered?

BEING BRUTALLY HONEST WITH YOU

Are you willing to have no barriers?

We are taught to believe that the judgements, barriers and walls we put up will protect us, but in truth, they hide us from ourselves.

Creating your own financial reality is about having an awareness of what actually is and then choosing what will create more for you. You have to be willing to have no judgement, no barriers, and total vulnerability. From there, you begin to see what is possible for you that you have been refusing to acknowledge.

TOOL: TURN YOUR WRONGNESS INTO STRONGNESS

▸ What if your wrongness is actually your strongness? Anywhere you think you are wrong is where you are just refusing to be strong. Look at what you decided is wrong about you. Write it down. Take a look and ask, "What strongness is this that I am not acknowledging?"

▸ You being you is one of the most attractive things in the world. When you judge you, you are not being you.

QUESTIONS

° If I were being me, what would I choose?

° If I were being me, what would I create?"

WHO AM I BEING RIGHT NOW? ME, OR SOMEONE ELSE?

What Would You Truly Like to Have?

Part of being vulnerable is also about being brutally honest about what you would like to have in your life. If you keep it hidden and secret from yourself, or pretend that you do not desire what you actually want, you have no chance of actually creating and choosing greater and having a life you truly enjoy.

TOOL: WRITE DOWN WHAT YOU TRULY DESIRE IN LIFE

▸ Are you willing to be so honest with yourself that you admitted what you would truly like to have in life, even if it makes no sense to anyone else? Write out a list of everything you would like to have in your life (use the questions below to help you). If nothing were impossible, what would you choose? Take a look at your list and ask. "What is it going to take to generate and create this with ease?"

QUESTIONS

- What would I like to create in my life?
- If I could have and be and do and create anything, what would I like to choose?
- What have I decided is impossible that I would truly like to have?
- What is the most ridiculous or inconceivable thing I could ask for?
- What is it I would like to request of the universe and demand of myself?

TRUSTING THAT YOU KNOW

You always knew, even when it didn't work out.

Have you ever known that something wasn't really going to work out the way you would like, but you did it anyway?

TOOL: ACKNOWLEDGE YOUR KNOWING

▸ Write down all the times you did something you knew you shouldn't and it worked out exactly as you knew it would. Write down all the times something worked out and you knew all along that it would, no matter what anyone else said. Acknowledge that no matter how it worked out, you always knew.

QUESTIONS

* What do I know about money that I have never given myself the chance to acknowledge, or was made wrong for?

If money was never the issue, what would you choose?

You have to ask yourself questions every day if you want to change things and if you want to create a financial future that works for you. Every day is new, there are always more possibilities available. All you have to do is ask.

QUESTIONS

* If money weren't the issue, what would I choose?
* What would I like to create in the world?
* Which of those could I begin to institute right now?
* Who would I have to talk to?
* What would I have to do?
* Where would I have to go?
* What choices could I make today to start creating my own financial reality?

PART TWO: MONEY COME, MONEY COME, MONEY COME!
Chapter 4: Ten things that will make the money come (and come and come)

1. Ask questions that invite money
2. Know exactly how much money you need to live – joyfully
3. Have money
4. Acknowledge you
5. Do what you love
6. Be aware of what you think, say and do
7. Stop being vested in the outcome
8. Give up believing in success, failure, needs & wants
9. Have allowance
10. Be willing to be out of control

Chapter 5: Ask questions that invite money

Questions are the invitation to receive, which allows money to show up. If you don't ask, you can't receive.

If you start a question with "Why" or "How", most often you are not really asking a question. If you are looking for a particular answer (or you can already predict an answer to the question) – guess what? You are not actually asking a question!

Here are examples of questions that will invite money.

- What could show up that would work out greater than I could imagine?

- What did I choose to create with this, and what other choices do I have?

- What's right about me that I am not getting?

- What can I be or do different each day to become more aware of the choices, possibilities and contributions that are available to me in every moment?

Start asking for the money, now!

The target here is to have more ease with asking for money. What if asking for money was actually fun for you? How much *fun* could you have asking for money to show up in all kinds of ways?

TOOL: PRACTICE ASKING FOR THE MONEY

- Stand in front of the mirror and ask, "Can I have the money now please?" Say it over and over.

- When you have a client who needs to pay you, or someone owes you money on an invoice, ask, "How would you like to pay for that?"

Use questions daily to invite money

Keep asking questions. No matter what shows up - ask for more, ask for greater. What if asking questions became so natural to you that you become an unstoppable, walking, talking invitation for possibilities with money?

QUESTIONS

- What else is possible?
- How does it get any better than this? (Ask when good and bad things show up)
- What would I like my financial reality to be like?
- What would I have to be or do different to create that?
- What can I be or do different today, to generate more money right away?
- What can I put my attention on today that will increase my money inflows?
- What can I add to my life today, to create more revenue streams right away?
- Who or what else could contribute to me having more money in my life?
- Where can I use my money so that it makes more money for me?
- If money was not the issue, what would I choose?
- If I were choosing just for me, just for fun, what would I choose?
- Who else? What else? Where else?
- Can I have the money now please?

Chapter 6: Know Exactly How Much Money You Need to Live - Joyfully!

You need to know exactly what it costs to run your life with joy, or you will not be able to effectively apply all of these wonderful tools because you will not have the clarity you need to move forward.

TOOL: WRITE DOWN WHAT IT COSTS YOU TO LIVE JOYFULLY

▸ Have a detailed look at how much it costs to run your life. If you have a business, do this for your business too.

▸ Write down your expenses. If you have a profit and loss statement or some sort of report from your bookkeeper, use that to figure out what it costs you to run your business or your life each month.

▸ Add up all your current debts. If you have around $20,000 or less in debt, divide it by 12 and add that in. If it's over $20,000 of debt, divide it by 24 months or more if you like. Just include that in the list.

▸ Write down what it costs to do the things you do for fun.

▸ Add it all together.

▸ Add 10% for your 10 percent account.

▸ And then, add another 20 percent, just for the fun of it. Because life is about having fun!

▸ Have a look at the amount you get. This is the actual amount you need to run your life each month.

▸ Ask questions. Demand that amount of money shows up and more.

▸ Do this exercise every six to 12 months, because as your life changes, your expenses and your desires and your requirements financially will also change.

QUESTIONS

- What would it take to create this amount of money *and more*, with total ease?
- What else can I add to my life?
- What else can I create?

TOOL #1 FOR HAVING MONEY: THE 10% ACCOUNT

Put away 10 percent of everything you earn.

You are putting it away as an honouring of you. Remember, this is not logical or linear. Energetically, the universe starts to contribute to you as well and you start to have money show up in the most random places.

TOOL #2 FOR HAVING MONEY: CARRY CASH

Carry around the amount of cash that you think a wealthy person would carry.

What does it create for you, seeing a large amount of cash in your wallet every time you open it? Does it contribute a sense of wealth? Is it fun? Try it and see.

If you have a point of view about carrying a lot of money on you because you think you will lose it or have it stolen, ask, "How much money would I need to carry on me so that I am willing to be aware of it at all times?"

TOOL #3 FOR HAVING MONEY: BUY THINGS OF INTRINSIC VALUE

Items of intrinsic value retain or increase their value once purchased.

Things like gold, silver, platinum, antiques, rare items have intrinsic value.

Consider purchasing liquid assets (things of value easily sold for cash) that also have an aesthetic beauty that add to your life, that will contribute to creating a sense of wealth and luxury in your life as well as having monetary value.

> ### TOOL: EDUCATE YOURSELF ABOUT ITEMS OF VALUE AND WHAT CREATES A SENSE OF WEALTH FOR YOU
>
> ▸ Educate yourself about things of value that would be fun for you to have in your life. Is it fun for you to have cash as well as liquid assets? How much cash would you need to have in your life to have a greater sense of peace and abundance with money? What else could you add to your life to create a sense of aesthetics, abundance, luxury and wealth that expands every facet of your life and living?

Chapter 8: Acknowledge You

There are three ways you can begin acknowledging you more effectively:

* Acknowledge the *value* of you
* Acknowledge what is *easy* for you to do and be
* Acknowledging what you *create*

Don't wait for others to see your value

Are you waiting for others to acknowledge you so that you finally know what you have to offer is valuable?

What if you would be the one who recognises you are valuable, no matter what anyone else thinks?

> ### TOOL: WRITE DOWN THE GRATITUDE YOU HAVE FOR YOU
>
> ▸ Get a notebook and write down what you are grateful for about you - add at least three different things every day. Make the demand to perceive, know be and receive the greatness of you with more ease. Commit to you, and have your own back in this process.

- What is great about me that I have never acknowledged?
- What have I been refusing to acknowledge about me that if I acknowledged it would create my life as far more ease-filled and joyful?

What is easy for you that you have never acknowledged?

What do you find easy to do? What do you find easy that you think has no value?

TOOL: WRITE DOWN WHAT IS EASY FOR YOU TO BE AND DO

- Start writing down the things you find easy, and truly be aware of them. Get the energy of what it is like to do those things that are easy. Acknowledge how brilliant you are!
- Ask that energy to show up in all the places you decided were not so easy. If you acknowledge that energy and ask it to grow in your life, it can and will.

- What else can I acknowledge about me that I did not think was of value?

Do you acknowledge your creations, or do you dismiss them?

How much are you actually creating in your life that you dismiss? What if you could be totally present with everything that occurs and everything that is created in your life - and receive it all, with gratitude? Notice the energy and sense of possibility that would be created in life with an acknowledgment like, "I created something really awesome today."

QUESTIONS

- What would it take to receive this money in my life, and have total gratitude for it, and me?
- Where else can I acknowledge my ability to create?
- What if I truly enjoyed my creation?
- How much fun can I have and what else can I now create?

Chapter 9: Do What You Love

When you include more of what you love doing, you will keep inviting the money to come play.

What Do You Love Doing?

You have to start looking at the things you love to do.

TOOL: MAKE A LIST OF EVERYTHING YOU LOVE DOING

- Get out a notepad and start writing down everything you love doing.
- Keep adding to it over the next days and weeks.
- Then take a look - are you doing enough of what you love?
- Ask some questions.

QUESTIONS

- Which of these could I create revenue streams with right away? (Notice if one, or a few jump out at you, what if you started with those ones?)

- What would I have to do and who would I have to talk to and where would I have to go to start creating these as a reality, right away?

- How much fun can I have creating this?

WHAT ELSE CAN YOU ADD?

You don't have to be on one track. You can have multiple streams or tracks going. What if you could create as many as you like? There is no limit to the amount of revenue streams you can ask for. How do you know which ones would be relevant? If it's fun for you, it's relevant.

Adding to your life will create more of what you desire, eliminating from your life will not.

If you begin to add more to your life, especially if you are creating with the things that you love, both the boredom and the overwhelm begin to melt away.

TOOL: TAKE A BIRD'S-EYE VIEW ON THINGS

> Practice taking that bird's-eye view now with a project or part of your life you tend to go into overwhelm with. Take a look and ask:

> "Could somebody else contribute to this?"

> "Could somebody else add something to this?"

> "Could somebody else do this better than me?"

> "What can I add to my life so that I have clarity and ease with all this and more?"

QUESTIONS

- If you are looking for more clients in your business, or you are getting bored with your work, ask: What else can I add here?
- If you are overwhelmed, ask: What can I add? What else can I create?

Do you create different from other people?

People project at you that you should finish one thing before you start another.

Is that true for you though? If you didn't judge the way you create as wrong, how much fun could you have with creating even more in your life?

QUESTIONS

- What works for me?
- Is it more fun to have lots of different things going on?
- If I could create my money and life any way I desire, what would I choose?

Chapter 10: Be Aware of What You Say, Think and Do

Start listening to everything that comes out of your mouth or pops into your head when it comes to money, especially those things that you tend to automatically believe are true and do not normally question - what if they are not actually true at all?

Wishing versus Creating.

How often have you put things on a kind of wish list, hoping that it will show up, but not taken action to start creating it?

Commitment is the willingness to give your time and energy to something that you demand to show up.

▸ Write down a list of what you desire to create in your life and your financial reality, instead of a wish list. Ask questions. And choose.

QUESTIONS

- What am I wishing for, rather than committing to the creation?
- If I were to be brutally honest, how much am I committed to my life right now? 10% or less? 15% or less? 20%?
- Am I willing to commit 100% to my life?
- Am I willing to commit to the creation of those things I desire?
- What is it going to take to create this?
- What do I have to put into action for that to occur?

Choosing in 10 second increments

Imagine if all your choices expired after 10 seconds. If you wanted to keep going a certain way, all you had to do was choose it again - you have to keep choosing it, consciously, every 10 seconds, so you better make sure it is something you actually desire to have! What if choice could truly be that easy? If you choose something and it does not work out, you don't have to waste time judging and reprimanding yourself for your last choice. You just have to choose again.

TOOL: LIVE 10 SECONDS AT A TIME

- Practice choosing in 10 second increments.
- Start with little things (standing, sitting, making a cup of tea, picking a flower etc.).
- Be fully present with each choice. Enjoy each choice. Do not make the choice significant, right, wrong or meaningful.
- Notice how your body feels, what occurs for you?

> Every time you choose, what if you could give yourself the gift of knowing that it is not stuck in stone?

Chapter 11: Stop Being Vested in the Outcome

When it comes to making choices in life, how vested are you in the outcome before you even get started? What if what you decided it must show up as, is a limitation? Stop being vested in the outcome, and ask for the awareness of which choices will expand your life and living. Allow yourself to get a sense of the *energy* of what each choice would create. Follow that energetic sense of what is more expansive, even if it does not make logical or cognitive sense to you.

TOOL: ASK TO RECEIVE THE ENERGY OF WHAT YOUR CHOICE WILL CREATE

> When you are looking at a choice to make, ask these two Questions
> If I choose this, what will my life be like in five years?
> If I don't choose this, what will my life be like in five years?

Indulge in it

Indulging in something means, "to yield to, or give oneself over to the pleasure of it."

Whenever you are considering a choice about something and you're not sure you wish to choose that, what if you would give yourself some time to indulge in it?

TOOL: INDULGE IN DIFFERENT CHOICES

> Look at something you are not sure that you wish to choose. For the next 3 days indulge in choosing it. When you indulge in something, you have way more awareness of the energy

that would be created or generated by choosing it. For the next 3 days, indulge in not choosing it. Which one is lighter for you?

* If I had no rules and regulations and no reference points, what would I create?

Chapter 12: Give Up Believing in Success, Failure, Needs & Wants

You already are successful, and if you want to change things in your life too, you can just change them. Where are you a success already that you have not acknowledged?

Falling and Failing

There is no such thing as failing. It's just your point of view. A choice that did not work out like you planned is not a failure, or wrongness. It is just different from what you thought.

TOOL: CHOOSE FOR AWARENESS AND DON'T TRY TO GET IT RIGHT

▶ Practice choosing to create awareness in your world. Do not make it about getting it right or wrong. What would you like to choose?

- What have you decided that you have to get right?
- Have you decided that your business / relationship / financial world has to be right?
- Have you decided that you have to make the right decision?
- Have you decided you have to avoid wrong decisions, or avoid falling and failing?
- What if you knew that choice creates awareness?
- What could this choice contribute to you that you are not yet aware of?

What if it's time to be as different as you truly are?

What if *you* are not a failure or wrong, just different?

TOOL: RECEIVE THE CONTRIBUTION OF YOUR "FAILURES"

- Write down what you believe are your failures in life. Once you have written them down, take a look, and for each one ask, "If I didn't judge this as a failure, what contribution can I receive from this?" and "What awareness did this create in my life that I wouldn't have otherwise?" Write down what pops into your head. Get out of the judgement of your choice and become aware of the contribution, the change, the awareness that it created for you.

- Write down what you believe are your "personal wrongnesses." Have a look at the list of things you judge yourself for being wrong for. Ask, "If I took away my judgement of wrongness around this, what strongness would this actually be?"

I don't need or want money - and neither do you!

Did you know that the original meaning of "want" in any dictionary prior to 1946 has 27 definitions that mean "to lack" and only *one* that means, "to desire"? Every time you say, "I want", you are actually saying, "I lack"!

TOOL: "I DON'T WANT MONEY"

» Practice saying every day, "I don't want money," out loud, at least 10 times in a row. Notice how it lightens things up? That lightness that you feel is the acknowledgment of what is true for you. Because, in truth, you don't lack of anything.

Necessity and Choice

We love to believe that we need things. But what if everything is actually a choice?

QUESTIONS

* What have I decided is a necessity?
* Is it really a necessity? Or is it a choice?
* What necessities can I now acknowledge are a choice?
* What if it's a choice I can make joyfully now?
* What would I like to create?

Chapter 13: Have and Be Allowance

Allowance is where you are the rock in the stream. All the points of view in this world about money wash right over you, but they don't carry you away with them. Allowance is not acceptance. It is not trying to make

154

believe everything is okay. You can draw your line in the sand. You can choose what works for you.

When people judge, it's not about you, it's about the judgments they have of them and of what they are not willing to create.

TOOL: WHAT IS YOUR JUDGEMENT OF YOU?

> If you find yourself judging someone or something, ask yourself what judgement you have of you in regards to this person or thing. See if it starts to lighten up. Judgement is not real and allowance creates possibilities.

QUESTIONS

- What would it take to be willing to receive the judgements (good and bad) that others have of me?
- What if I were willing to receive it all with ease?

Are you willing to be in allowance of you?

Most of the judgements we have about ourselves, 99% of them are ones we have picked up from the people around us. They are not actually real or true.

TOOL: DON'T JUDGE YOUR JUDGEMENTS, ENJOY THEM, THEN CHOOSE AGAIN!

- When you are judging you, acknowledge: "Right now I am choosing to judge me. I am going to enjoy that for a minute, and then I am going to choose to stop judging me."
- You can choose to judge you, and you can choose to stop judging you.
- When you are ready to stop judging you, ask questions.

- What's right about me I am not getting?"
- What if nothing I have ever been or done was wrong?
- And what if nothing about me is wrong?
- What gift in my life would having total allowance for me actually be?
- What kindness can I be for me by not judging myself today?

Don't try to change people.

The only person you can change is you, no one else. If you try to get people to choose what you want them to choose, they end up resisting you and hating you for it. Let other people choose what they choose, and keep choosing what you choose.

- Am I judging my partner's / family's / friends' choices?
- What allowance can I have for them and their choice?
- What would I like to choose for me now that I haven't yet chosen?

Chapter 14: Be Willing To Be Out Of Control

How much have you made the money in your life small enough for you to control?

What if you could create your life, business and different revenue streams by expanding your awareness and *letting go* of what you have been trying to control?

What if you could create brilliantly from the chaos?

Remember how creating money is not linear? You are not linear either! What if you could create however you desire and require to create, even if it appears totally chaotic to others? What if you would give up trying to control your life and started to just create it? Remember, you are not alone in the universe, the universe will contribute to you creating everything you desire, so ask for more.

TOOL: GIVE UP CONTROL AND LET GO

▸ For the next week, try letting go of the reins of everything you've been holding onto so tightly. Let go of the things you've been trying to control and see if something new can show up. Ask lots of questions.

QUESTIONS

* What questions do I need to ask to create all of this with ease?
* Who or what else can I add to my business and life?
* What would it take for this to be easy?
* What requires my attention today?
* What do I need to work on now to create this?

Chapter 15: A Note About Cash Flow

What if creating cash flow is really just about playing with possibilities?

> **TOOL: PAY ATTENTION TO YOUR CASH FLOW AND ASK MORE QUESTIONS**
>
> ▶ Look at the cash flow you currently have or do not have. Take time to give it your attention and ask more questions every day. Start to educate yourself about money.

QUESTIONS

- What would it take to have continuous cash flow in my life?
- How many revenue and creation streams can I create?
- What do I want to play with?
- What brings me joy?
- What am I curious about?
- What else exists out there in the world with regards to money that would be fun for me to discover?

TWO MORE ACCESS CONSCIOUSNESS TOOLS YOU CAN ADD TO EXPONENTIALISE EVERYTHING

The difference that Access Consciousness has created in my life is exponential.

Access Consciousness is a massive tool-kit for creating change in your life, to ultimately change the way you function so that nothing is limited and there is more and more space to choose anything you desire.

It is not just the questions, concepts and 'doing' tools that Access Consciousness offers that really allow you to change things, it is the clearing of the *underlying energy* of all of the points of views and conclusions and judgments that keep things stuck and unchangeable in our lives. If we could work it all out with our logical mind we would have everything we ever desired, it's the insane points of view that lock us up. The clearing statement works to change all of that and more.

There are two tools for clearing and changing that underlying energy that I highly recommend you use in conjunction with the rest of the tools in this book: The Access Consciousness® Clearing Statement, and Access Bars®.

The Clearing Statement is a verbal process that you can add to your questions that clear the energy of where you currently feel limited or stuck. Access Bars is a hands-on body process that allows you to dissipate the stuck component of the thoughts, feelings and emotions that are locked into your body and your points of view (your life).

I read so many books years ago where I was looking to change an area of my life, and when I read people's stories it was more annoying than anything else, as I was like, "Well that's great, and how do you do that? How do you change it?" This book is different. You have my stories, you have questions and tools and you also have clearings to run with the Clearing Statement. This changed everything for me. My desire is for you to know that these tools exist and that you can change any area of your life that you *think* is not working for you. The choice is totally yours.

THE ACCESS CONSCIOUSNESS® CLEARING STATEMENT

The Clearing Statement is one of the foundational tools in Access Consciousness that I would describe as the "magic" that occurs. It's basically about the energy. When you ask a question and then run the Clearing Statement, you are changing, destroying and un-creating all the places where you have created a point of view that is stopping you from having, being or choosing something different.

The Clearing Statement is basically designed to change all of those places where you have thoughts, feelings, emotions, limitations, judgements and conclusions that should not exist, and create more of the sense of play and joy and have something different show up, to create more awareness so you will have more possibilities available to you.

The full Clearing Statement is: *Right and wrong, good and bad, POD and POC, all 9, shorts, boys and beyonds®.*

It is a shorthand phrase for all different kinds of energies that you are clearing. The beauty of the Clearing Statement is you don't have to understand it or even have to remember the entire statement. You can just say "POD and POC", or "All that stuff," or even "That energy from that strange book I just read." Because it is about the energy, not the words, it will still run.

Below is an abridged explanation of the Clearing Statement words. If you would like more information you can go to www.theclearingstatement.com

RIGHT AND WRONG, GOOD AND BAD

This part of the statement is shorthand for, "What have I decided is right, good, perfect and correct about this? What have I decided is wrong, mean, vicious, terrible, bad, and awful about this?"

POD and POC

POD stands for the Point Of Destruction of the thoughts, feelings and emotions immediately preceding the decisions to lock that judgement, point of view or energy in place, and all the ways you have been destroying yourself in order to keep it in existence. POC stands for the

Point Of Creation of the thoughts, feelings and emotions immediately preceding your decision to lock the energy in place.

"POD and POC" is also an abbreviated way of saying the clearing statement.

When you "POD and POC" something, it is like pulling the bottom card out of a house of cards. The whole thing falls down.

All 9

"All 9" stands for the nine different ways you have created this item as a limitation in your life. They are the layers of thoughts, feelings, emotions and points of view that create the limitation as solid and real.

Shorts

"Shorts" is the short version of a much longer series of questions that include: What's meaningful about this? What's meaningless about this? What's the punishment for this? What's the reward for this?

Boys

We have this point of view that if we keep peeling back the layers of the onion we will get to the core of the issue, but how often do you find you never really get there? "Boys" stands for energetic structures called nucleated spheres that we misidentify as the onions we thought we had to peel. Nucleated spheres are like the bubbles that come out of a kids' bubble pipe. We keep trying to pop the bubbles thinking that is dealing with the issue, but it's the kid blowing air into the pipe creating the bubbles. Remove the kid, the bubbles stop. This is the energy that is referred to that is collectively called "the boys."

Beyonds

These are feelings or sensations you get that stop your heart, stop your breath, or stop your willingness to look at possibilities. Beyonds are what occur when you are in shock – like when you receive an unexpectedly big phone bill. They are usually feelings and sensations, rarely emotions, and never thoughts.

HOW THE CLEARING STATEMENT WORKS

The first time I heard the clearing statement I was at an introduction night to Access Consciousness, and when I heard the facilitator of the class say the statement, I thought, "What the hell is this guy talking about? I have no idea what this is!" What I did notice was, the next morning when I woke up, things had changed for me.

I had ordered my life into existence: up at 6.30am, at the gym by 7am (and I must go to gym or otherwise I will judge myself continuously all day), at the office by 9am, running my business Monday to Friday and staying back late and doing this and that. It all had to look a certain way. And that's how I thought it would always be.

The morning after that class, sitting in bed, I realised, "Oh I haven't even gotten up to go to the gym," and I felt this sense of space, and I still didn't quite know what had occurred.

The facilitator from the evening before rang me and said, "Hey I am just ringing to see how you are going," and I said, "What the hell did you do to me last night?" He asked, "What do you mean?" I explained that it felt to me like my entire life had just changed. Everything I had decided I had to do was no longer relevant. It was like there was now a different possibility available, and I had no idea what that was. But the joy of it was, *I didn't feel like I had to work it out.* There was a sense of play in my world that I had not experienced since I was a child.

One thing I knew was that whatever this facilitator had been talking about at this introductory class to Access, it worked. And I desired more. I immediately asked, "So what are you doing next? When's the next class?" The facilitator told me what the next class was, but it was Christmas time so no one would want to do a class at this time of year. I asked, "How many people do you need to do this class?" and he said, "Four." I said, "Done." Within three days I had four people come to a class and we did it right between Christmas and New Year.

That was the demand in my world to have more of whatever this was, *now*. I had been seeking for so many years – through spiritual avenues, through drugs, through travelling all around the world, I was seeking something more. In every aspect, I had looked for whatever this was. I realised later that what this was showing me was *me*. I had always looked elsewhere, outside of me, as the source of change and what I was starting to realise was, I was the source for change.

HOW TO USE THE CLEARING STATEMENT

To use the Clearing Statement, you first ask a question. When you ask a question, it brings up an energy. It might even bring up particular thoughts, feelings or emotions, and it might not. You then ask to clear that energy that comes up by running the Clearing Statement. For example:

"What judgements do I have about creating money?" Everything that is (ie. All the energy that brings up) I now destroy and un-create it all. *Right and wrong, good and bad, POD and POC, All 9, shorts, boys and beyonds."*

In a class, the facilitator asks you a question and then asks, "Everything that brings up, would you be willing to destroy and un-create it all?" And then runs the Clearing Statement. The reason we do it this way, is because it is up to you how much you let go and are willing to change. The Clearing Statement will not clear anything that is working for you, or that you don't desire to change. It will only clear what you are willing to let go of and desire to let go of.

At the end of this chapter, I have included a list of processes (questions with the Clearing Statement) you can run. The idea is that you run them over and over to keep clearing more and more energy to gain more ease, space and choice in that area.

ACCESS BARS®

Access Bars are 32 points on your head that when touched lightly start to dissipate the thoughts, feelings and emotions you have on topics such as healing, sadness, joy, sexuality, body, aging, creativity, control, money, to name a few. I am sure you don't have any points of view about any of these topics, do you?

I strongly suggest getting your Bars run. It allows your body to be included in the change you are creating. And the more you include your body in the process of changing your life, the more joyful and ease-filled it will be.

The first time I got my Bars run, it created a space for me where I didn't seem to have a strong point of view about anything. There was more availability to choose something different. The more you run the Bars, the greater that space becomes.

Another way you can use the Bars to assist you in changing things is, while you are having your money Bar run, you can talk about what comes up for you with money. And what happens is it starts to press the delete button on what you decided money is; all the points of view you bought about money, all the points of view from your family, friends, culture, where you were born and so on, and start to create your own financial reality.

Find a practitioner, or even attend a class. Learning Access Bars is a one-day workshop and you spend the day running Bars – receiving two sessions and gifting two sessions. You will walk out feeling completely different.

For more information, go to www.bars.accessconsciousness.com

ACCESS CONSCIOUSNESS MONEY PROCESSES

The following list of money processes are what you can run to clear the energy that stops you from having greater possibilities. The more you run these processes, the more change you get. They are also available in audio (you can download for free from the website www.gettingoutofdebtjoyfully.com/bookGIFT), which you can play on a repetitive loop on your mp3 player or phone. You can even play this at almost inaudible volume while you sleep. They will work even more dynamically without your cognitive mind in the way. Have fun! Remember: Getting Out of Debt Joyfully!

What does money mean to you? Everything that is will you destroy and uncreate it? **Right and wrong, good and bad, POD and POC, all 9, shorts, boys and beyonds.**®

What have you decided and concluded is right about money? Everything that is will you destroy and uncreate it? **Right and wrong, good and bad, POD and POC, all 9, shorts, boys and beyonds.**®

What have you decided and concluded is wrong about money? Everything that is will you destroy and uncreate it? **Right and wrong, good and bad, POD and POC, all 9, shorts, boys and beyonds.**®

Get the amount of money you're currently earning and times it by 2, perceive the energy of that. Everything that doesn't allow that to show up will you destroy and uncreate it? **Right and wrong, good and bad, POD and POC, all 9, shorts, boys and beyonds.**®

Now get the amount of money you're currently earning and times it by 5, perceive the energy of that. Everything that doesn't allow that to show up will you destroy and uncreate it? **Right and wrong, good and bad, POD and POC, all 9, shorts, boys and beyonds.**®

Now times it by ten. Everything that is will you destroy and uncreate it? **Right and wrong, good and bad, POD and POC, all 9, shorts, boys and beyonds.**®

Now times it by 50. Now earn 50 times the amount of money that you currently earn. All of the judgements, projections, separations, everything you've decided and concluded could occur, will you destroy and uncreate it? **Right and wrong, good and bad, POD and POC, all 9, shorts, boys and beyonds.**®

Now it's 100 times. Everything that is will you destroy and uncreate it? **Right and wrong, good and bad, POD and POC, all 9, shorts, boys and beyonds.**®

What energy do I have to be or do today to generate more money right away? Everything that is, times a godzillion (that's a number so big that only God knows!), will you destroy and uncreate it? **Right and wrong, good and bad, POD and POC, all 9, shorts, boys and beyonds.**®

Where are you limiting yourself and what you can create because you have made it about money and not the fun of it? Everything that is, times a godzillion, will you destroy and uncreate it? **Right and wrong, good and bad, POD and POC, all 9, shorts, boys and beyonds.**®

What generative, energy, space and consciousness can my body and I be that would allow every day to be a celebration of living? Everything that is, times a godzillion, will you destroy and uncreate it? **Right and wrong, good and bad, POD and POC, all 9, shorts, boys and beyonds.®**

What are you proving with money? What are you proving with no money? Everything that is, times a godzillion, will you destroy and uncreate it? **Right and wrong, good and bad, POD and POC, all 9, shorts, boys and beyonds.®**

What creation of money are you using to validate other people's realities and invalidate yours are you choosing? Everything that is, times a godzillion, will you destroy and uncreate it? **Right and wrong, good and bad, POD and POC, all 9, shorts, boys and beyonds.®**

What have you decided about money that if you didn't decide it about money would create a totally different reality and cash flow? Everything that is, times a godzillion, will you destroy and uncreate it? **Right and wrong, good and bad, POD and POC, all 9, shorts, boys and beyonds.®**

What do you love about hating money? What do you hate about loving money? Everything that is, times a godzillion, will you destroy and uncreate it? **Right and wrong, good and bad, POD and POC, all 9, shorts, boys and beyonds.®**

What do you have against being rich and wealthy? Everything that is, times a godzillion, will you destroy and uncreate it? **Right and wrong, good and bad, POD and POC, all 9, shorts, boys and beyonds.®**

What have you decided money is that it isn't that keeps you from making lots of money? Everything that is, times a godzillion, will you destroy and uncreate it? **Right and wrong, good and bad, POD and POC, all 9, shorts, boys and beyonds.®**

What secrets do you have with money? What are your dark, deep secrets? Everything that is, times a godzillion, will you destroy and uncreate it? **Right and wrong, good and bad, POD and POC, all 9, shorts, boys and beyonds.®**

Are you willing to work hard enough to be a Billionaire? Everything that is, times a godzillion, will you destroy and uncreate it? **Right and wrong, good and bad, POD and POC, all 9, shorts, boys and beyonds.®**

What judgment do you have of money, profit, business and success? Everything that is, times a godzillion, will you destroy and uncreate it? **Right and wrong, good and bad, POD and POC, all 9, shorts, boys and beyonds.®**

Everywhere you have decided that loads of money is inconceivable, will you destroy and uncreate it? Everything that is times a godzillion, will you destroy and uncreate it all? **Right and wrong, good and bad, POD and POC, all 9, shorts, boys and beyonds.®**

What energy, space and consciousness could you and your body be that would allow you to have too much money and never enough? Everything that is times a godzillion, will you destroy and uncreate it? **Right and wrong, good and bad, POD and POC, all 9, shorts, boys and beyonds.®**

How many of you create based on no money. You make money the source of creation rather than YOU as the source of creation? Everything that is times a godzillion, will you destroy and uncreate it? **Right and wrong, good and bad, POD and POC, all 9, shorts, boys and beyonds.®**

What do you know about investment that you have been refusing to acknowledge that if you acknowledged it would create you more money than you have ever dreamt of? Everything that is, times a godzillion, will you destroy and uncreate it? **Right and wrong, good and bad, POD and POC, all 9, shorts, boys and beyonds.®**

How many different revenue streams can you create? What other revenue streams could you play with? Where have you not allowed the random revenue streams to show up that could create more money than you ever thought possible? Everything that is, times a godzillion, will you destroy and uncreate it? **Right and wrong, good and bad, POD and POC, all 9, shorts, boys and beyonds.**®

What is it that you have that you are not willing to use to increase money, currency flows and revenue streams? Everything that is, times a godzillion, will you destroy and uncreate it all? **Right and wrong, good and bad, POD and POC, all 9, shorts, boys and beyonds.**®

Where are you quitting to create the lack of money you are choosing? Everything that is, will you destroy and uncreate it all? **Right and wrong, good and bad, POD and POC, all 9, shorts, boys and beyonds.**®

What have you made so vital about never ever, ever, ever, ever, ever having money that maintains the consistency of no change, no creation, no fun, no happiness? Everything that is times a godzillion, will you destroy and uncreate it all? **Right and wrong, good and bad, POD and POC, all 9, shorts, boys and beyonds.**®

What enthusiasm are you refusing that you truly could be choosing, that if you would choose it, would create more money than you ever thought was possible? Everything that is, will you destroy and uncreate it? **Right and wrong, good and bad, POD and POC, all 9, shorts, boys and beyonds.**®

Who or what are you refusing to lose that if you lost them would allow you to have too much money? Everything that is, will you destroy and uncreate it? **Right and wrong, good and bad, POD and POC, all 9, shorts, boys and beyonds.**®

What are you refusing to be that you could be, that if you would be it, would change your entire financial reality? Everything that is, will you destroy and uncreate it? **Right and wrong, good and bad, POD and POC, all 9, shorts, boys and beyonds.**®

What level of enthusiasm and the joy of living are you refusing that if you didn't refuse it, would change your entire financial reality? Everything that is, will you destroy and uncreate it? **Right and wrong, good and bad, POD and POC, all 9, shorts, boys and beyonds.**®

What have you been unwilling to receive that if you received it would create the money flows and the currency flows you know you deserve? Everything that doesn't allow that to show up will you destroy and uncreate it all? **Right and wrong, good and bad, POD and POC, all 9, shorts, boys and beyonds.**®

How much doubt are you using to create the lack of money you are choosing? Everything that is, will you destroy and uncreate it? **Right and wrong, good and bad, POD and POC, all 9, shorts, boys and beyonds.**®

What have you created with your life that you haven't been willing to acknowledge that if you did acknowledge it, could create way more? Everything that is, will you destroy and uncreate it? **Right and wrong, good and bad, POD and POC, all 9, shorts, boys and beyonds.**®

What are you now capable of creating that you have been unwilling to perceive, know, be and receive that if you would choose it would actualise as less work, more money and greater change in the world? Everything that is will you destroy and uncreate it? **Right and wrong, good and bad, POD and POC, all 9, shorts, boys and beyonds.**®

Part Four

Stories of Change

STORIES OF CHANGE

Sometimes when you read about how one person changed their reality with money, it can be easy to think, "Oh it was different for them, it was easier for them somehow, it probably won't work for me."

It truly doesn't matter where you are from, how old you are, how young you are, whether you have some money, a lot of money, or no money - your money situation does not have to look like it did in the past, or even how it does today; it can change, and it can expand.

I have a whole lot of people around me; wonderful, amazing people I know that did not always have the situation they have with money as they do now, and I was excited to be able to interview them, specifically to share it with you in this book.

All of these people either grew up or lived in situations where they struggled with money and had limited points of view about money – and they changed it. I hope their stories will inspire you and contribute to you knowing that changing debt and points of view around money does not have to be significant, it is just something in your life that you can change.

Note: The following interviews are edited transcripts. The full interviews were aired on The Joy of Business radio show. You can find and listen to the recorded episodes of the show in our archives at http://accessjoyofbusiness.com/radio-show/

INTERVIEW WITH CHRISTOPHER HUGHES

Taken from the Joy of Business internet radio show, "Getting Out of Debt Joyfully with Christopher Hughes" aired on 27th July 2016.

What was your life like when you were in debt? How did you function when you didn't have money? What were some of your key points of view?

Where I was functioning from and my key points of view around money at the time, were that it was too hard; that I didn't have the opportunities that other people had, or there just wasn't enough out there that I could make it work.

I thought that there was not enough money and not enough people that could help me with what I wanted to do, or that were interested enough in my products and services I was offering, or, you know, x, y and z reasons.

Was that closely linked to all the places where you were not willing to see the value of you, or the value of money?

Well, yes and no. It was the value of me but also, I made my situation the reason why I didn't have the money I required. And sometimes it was unreal how little I would have. Not only was there debt, but it would be like, "Wow, the gas tank is so close to empty and I've got 50 cents. Hmm. I'll slow down with my driving because I want to use less fuel. If I could just make sure I can get home."

It was like, "What can I do with a tin of tuna to make it interesting tonight?"— if I could afford tuna! But it was all about projecting the reasons on my situation. It's so funny, because in my life I've never really done that with anything before. I probably had more of a tendency to make myself wrong for something, but for some reason with money, I always said it was about the scenario I was in; the situation I was in, the circumstances surrounding me. That was my particular lens that I was looking through at the time.

So, it wasn't your fault? It was everybody else's fault that you had no money, that sort of thing? Or just how you were bought up?

Absolutely. I had to get really fed up, really frustrated and really annoyed with not having money to go, "Wait a minute. Why *am* I choosing this? Why am I blaming it on the scenario and situation?" I realised - through going through Access Consciousness classes and having a long hard look at the scenario - "Oh, that was actually the way my mum lived, who raised me." She had all the reasons in the world to blame it on too. She got married when she was 16 because she was pregnant, and it ended up she was 25 years of age and had 3 kids. The oldest of which was like 9. And only had high school, not any other education. And my father was quite a violent man. I remember her picking me up from my last day of kindergarten and we drove to another city to hide from him because he was so violent. And she worked at 7/11 convenience stores during the day and put herself through high school at night, so she could slowly build up and build up. But she did have a lot of points of view. I was raised around the scenario and the situation and your lot in life being to struggle, being hard. It was the hand that was dealt to you, not what you created.

Is there anything that you distinctly remember where you created the energy of avoiding, or ignorance, or it's always going to be perpetuating the debt?

My particular spin on that, or brand, was I was always travelling; I was a traveller. I was born in Canada in a small town but left as soon as I could because you did, unless you were pregnant, like my mother. So, I was always travelling and constantly reinventing myself and moving to the other side of the country for 4 years and then moving to Asia for a number of years, and moving here and there. And I never really had to establish myself anywhere or commit to building a life wherever I was.

So, yes, there would be lots of those envelopes arriving, going, "We're going to cut this service," or, "You didn't do this" and it never struck me as impacting my life, because I hadn't really committed to be there anyway; I just went "Oh well." I used to go through car after dodgy car; that was all I could afford and they would be the worst bombs you'd ever seen in your life.

I remember one broke down and I just sort of went "Oh," and I reached into the cup holder and grabbed the change that was there and put it in my pocket, and I left it on the side of the road and just walked away. Because it was the whole thing. I wasn't really willing to commit to having the life where I took care of myself and I took care of those things, and I covered all those expenses and honoured myself with not only covering the expenses, but having more for myself.

Actually, it was really funny; I have to tell the rest of the story walking away from that bomb. It wasn't just the change in the console of the car I took away with me. I took that, but also I was living in the Sunshine Coast in Queensland at the time, which is about 2 hours from Brisbane, which is where the car died, and I'd been in Brisbane and I'd bought a Christmas present for Brendon, Simone's partner, and I took it and the change – it was a set of pots and pans because he was really starting to get into cooking – and I took the change and used it to get a train from Brisbane back to the Sunshine Coast, and I remember I had nothing and I got to the Sunshine Coast. The train station was still 35-45 minutes away from where I was living and I went, "I actually don't know how to get home." I had no money.

So how did you get home?

"I had so little money I had to call everyone I knew to find someone who would get me the last 30 minutes home."

Recently, you took your first ride in a Tesla car. When you got out you said, "Okay, I think I want a new car. I think it's time for an upgrade."

Currently a Tesla is about $AUD 220,000. When you look at something like that in your life… where would that sort of thing have sat in your universe years ago? What was your point of view? And what is your point of view now?

Years ago, and not that many years ago actually, it would have been, "Oh my god. Don't even bother." But I would have done that with a $50,000 car. So a $220,000 car would just be ridiculous and absurd and why would you even bother, don't even look at a car like that; don't even walk next to it. Not now. I'll be like, "Okay. To create that for myself it will take a little bit of negotiations and working around and I would need to see what I can get in terms of finance, but I could probably handle it."

Recently, I went to a shop and I bought three of these beautiful shirts, and they were about $500 each, which again, previously in debt that would have been like, "Woah, what are you doing?" But I bought all of them that were in my size. I would have bought more if they'd had more. And that was such a different point of view and paradigm. It was like, "Yeah. Why not?" That was one of the major things I've noticed with not being in debt, is that there's this huge area in my life where I no longer function from a limitation.

What places in your life did you change to create that? What demand did you have to make? What tools did you use to change that so that you no longer function from a limitation?

There were a few things. I mean, there's this tool in Access Consciousness that Gary Douglas introduced to me, which was the 10% account. Where for every dollar that comes into your life, you take 10% and you set it aside as an honouring of you; you never spend it, you don't use it on bills, you don't use it for whatever. But for me, that was tricky. I could never rationalise to myself that if I had that red envelope come, saying, "We're going to cut your electricity," that I wouldn't use my 10% for that. So what I did was, I started to trick myself into having money, and my way of doing that was buying silver.

177

Silver is a tradeable commodity on the stock exchange. They have a spot price daily for where the market is with silver. It's currency. So I would buy these things with my 10% that were worth money, but you couldn't use it to pay a bill. I mean, you could take it in and get it exchanged for currency or whatever, and you might lose money or make money on the trade, but that's really inconvenient. And that little buffer between how long it would take for me to liquidate the item to paying the bill, always gave me enough time to go, "No wait. I'd really like to have that in my life." And, the cool thing for me too, because sometimes with my 10% I'd buy a spoon for $40 and sometimes I'd buy a kilo of silver, which today is something like $AUD 900. And after a while, those smaller increments and larger increments really started to add up. I remember applying for my mortgage a year or two ago, and had no idea whether I would qualify for a mortgage or not; whether the bank would really want to lend me any money. And we went around the house adding up all the silver and gold and these sorts of things, and we had close to $150,000 just in silver.

Based on that, the bank was like, "Yeah, we'll lend you the money. You're asset rich." And I went, "Oh. That's new." So that 10% account was probably the biggest key thing for me, to trick myself to having money, because in my life I was always great at creating it, not so good at having it.

Did you start your 10% account straight away, or what was your point of view about this tool initially?

I didn't start straight away, to be totally honest. I had been taking Access Consciousness classes for probably, oh, total now around 10 years and I had major points of view about the 10% thing, because I was like, "Whatever." Because a bill would come in and I would say to myself, "There's no way it's going to create more to have this money in the bank when I've got this whopping bill that I don't know how to pay."

Gary Douglas would always say, "Ask and you will receive. Ask for the money to show up. Don't spend your 10%. That's an honouring of you. Ask for the money to show up." And I would constantly put myself behind the bill; make the bill more important and pay it first. And when I started buying these "financial instruments" - the silver, antiques etc - as I call them, that were not immediately liquid, it was harder [to spend it]; and I had this energy of wealth slowly creep into my life. And now, I look at my house and I go, "Hmm. Everything is super valuable."

My husband and I, we were looking at this auction the other day of a lady's collection of things; paintings and silver and jewellery and furniture that she'd collected over her life, and they were auctioning it. And we looked at our stuff and said, "We're in our mid-30s and we have better stuff!" More valuable stuff. Not from a judgement, but it made us go, "Wow. We're really quickly amassing wealth!" And it's not about saving and it's not about the money; it's about a joy that it brings to us. And it really started with that 10% account.

For every dollar that comes into your life that you earn, take 10% and put it aside as an honouring of you. If you want to buy gold and silver and things that you know won't lose money, great. Go for it. Or, if you're a little more disciplined than I was, just have it, in an account, set aside, or in a sock drawer or whatever it is for you, where you have that money; you *have* the money. Because that was the hard part for me.

When you tell these stories of how you went from having no money to having money - from leaving the car on the side of the road with a pocket of change to $150,000 of silver in your home... it is not that long ago that you had these "poverty stricken" days.

If you actually did the math it probably was 4 years ago. So to have 4 years to go from that to looking around my house; not only do I have a house, yes it is mortgaged, but we have a house, and two cars and heaps of valuable antiques and a box of unset gems around the house and a pile of silver and a bunch of gold and it's a different world.

What made you want to get out of debt?

It occurred to me at some point, that with having debt and not allowing myself to have money, I was severely limiting what I could create in the world. The change that was possible for me to inspire in others and, I mean, it wasn't about having a nice car and a fancy house and a lifestyle, it was more about realising that you can actually influence the world and change it if you have the resources to do it.

Was there anybody that was an inspiration for you to create that change?

You, Simone, were a massive inspiration for me to create that change. You've been my friend for 10 years. The generosity that I have seen you be with people, not from a "make them like me" place or an "I'm better than you, I will take care of you" place of superiority, but from a "kingdom of we" kind of energy, where it's all about everybody having and really contributing to everybody and what they're trying to build. I don't want to use the word "support," but what I see you do is, money for you has never been the cheap motivation; yeah, it's fun, but it's what you can do with it that is really inspiring.

I have a good relationship as well with Gary Douglas and these are all people that don't function with money the way you are told you are supposed to; you know, in movies, in the media, in the way this reality tells you are supposed to be with money. I saw a different possibility with money that made me go, "Huh! I want that." It's not about having big rings on my fingers, it's about what I can create.

Now that you actually have money, what would you say your point of view about money is now?

There are a few things that jump to mind immediately. Now, money is just fun. Money is, like - wow, when I say these things, I can sense people listening going, "Eergh, it's so easy for you!"

I remember once upon a time going to these yoga classes, and I've never been a naturally flexible person physically. And I remember going up to my yoga teacher saying, "I can't do this one move. I can't bend like that." And she would say to me, "That's tension. You should let it go." And I would want to punch her in the face, or strangle her with the lycra she was wearing; sorry for the mental imagery. But, what money is now is...I realised it is really just a point of view that creates having it or not having it, or, it's sort of like if you want a relationship and you haven't got one. Once you have one you realise, "Oh, hang on. It's not the impossibility and the fantasy and the dream I made it out to be." Once you have money, it's not like you never have to face any issues any more or never have any problems in your life.

In any case, your life gets bigger, if you are willing for it to get bigger; the options, the possibilities, the doors that can open to you if you are willing, can grow, if that's your choice. Now, I realise that money was never the answer. There are so many people out there without money or who are in debt, going, "If only I had money and a partner and, and, and..." You've built this list of things you'd like to have as though they're the answer and they're going to completely create your life. But that's not it at all. Money is just a fuel; it's just a tool that gets you where you are going. That's my appreciation of it now, and the less I have a point of view of it and the more I make the creation of it just about fun, the easier it is.

So, what else would you say has changed the most with your point of view around money now? What's some of that energy that people could change, or what's a tool that people can use to help them change their point of view around money?

Probably the best advice I could give or tool that I could give is, in actual fact, the problem never is money; it's never money itself that is creating the issue, that is creating the lack or whatever drama it is that you are having in your life. There's plenty of it out there. It's like, you know, one of your favourite movies, and one of mine, is *Auntie Mame* with Rosalind

Russell, and she says, "The universe is a banquet but most poor suckers are out there starving to death."

It's there. There isn't actually a finite amount of money out there in the universe. I deal in antiques, and it is an industry where most people are operating from scarcity. They have a point of view that the industry is dying; people don't desire what we have anymore.

I deal in antique furniture and jewellery, silver, paintings, Chinese art, African art, you name it. And when the opportunity first arrived on my doorstep I went, "Oh my god. I can't think of anything more boring!" And, gosh, it's been anything but. In that industry, I deal with so many antique dealers, across Australia particularly. A lot of them are functioning from this incredible scarcity; that there's not enough money, people aren't interested, it's getting too hard, auction houses are taking away from the retailers and making it too difficult for them to get the prices they want. It really all is a point of view.

If you want a tool to change your situation: your point of view creates your reality. Ask yourself, and have a good look, "What *is* my point of view about money?" What is your point of view about *you* with regards to money? Have a look at some of those things, start asking yourself and run with it. There's a fabulous book in Access Consciousness called How To Become Money. I think it's like $30, unless it's changed, but it's a fabulous workbook where you get to ask yourself these questions and you can totally, 180 degrees, change your whole financial situation just with that one investment in that book. And why not? I mean, all it can do is help.

When you'd like to do something or have something that you don't have enough cash for, what do you do? What tools do you use to create it, or how do you approach that situation?

Aha. Good question. I like this question because, no matter how much money you have or don't have, you can still always be asking and looking for more. So it isn't necessarily just about being in debt or not having enough. Like, for me right now, buying that Tesla car that we talked about earlier for $220,000 as an example, that would require for me to do some juggling or some rearranging or some creation on my part to actually make that happen. So, in terms of tools that I would use to do that, one of the greatest pieces of advice I have ever received around money and finances is, get really clear on what it costs to run your life. Sit down with a pen and paper and write down what are your outgoings; what are your expenses. So, you have your rent, you have your phone bill, you have, "I like to go out for a drink,"; not just the bare bones basics but what do you really spend in your life.

I did this once in a business when I first started there, and I asked the bookkeeper to bring me a copy of the profit and loss and I sat down with her and I went through all of it and figured out exactly where all the money in the organisation was going. And it created such amazing awareness for me about the financial situation of the company. So how clear are you about your own financial situation? I teach classes a lot on sales and marketing and I've been here in Copenhagen with you Simone doing one, and it's been such a great gift for me, but the piece of advice I gave in class as well was for people to get really clear on their businesses and their lives about where they are financially.

In marketing there's this old saying that goes, "50% of my advertising budget is wasted. I'm just not sure which it is." And, with people's finances it's the same thing. It is surprising how many people are out there that have no idea how much money they actually make in a month and how much they are actually spending. So if I wanted to create the money to get there, establish the lay of the land and know where I'm at and what I would need to create to get there. It's not about building the steps a, b, c, d in a linear fashion like that, but know, "Where I am at now and what's my target?" For me, having a target is so helpful. Say I have some particular targets - like opening a second location is one of the things I am looking at for my business - I figure out what that will cost and I ask for that to show up and then follow the energy that allows that to take place. Again, it's not about really linear steps of how I am going to do it and how much I am going to need to make and crack the whip in my store so that everyone meets the sales target. It's more about going, "Okay, now I have the awareness... what's it going to take to create that?"

Christopher, can you tell me a little bit more about where people can find you and what you are doing? Because I know you do some amazing classes called The Elegance of Living.

I do facilitate a group of classes called *The Elegance of Living*, all about teaching you about different aspects of wealth and living with what I like to call the trappings of money; although "trappings" seems to be a loaded word, I think it's still a bit fun. And learning more about antiques and art and how they can add to your life and also add to your wealth. My partner and I, we started this because we took the change from our change jar at home and we had $500 and we went to auctions and bought a bunch of stuff and started selling it and quickly took the change in that jar and turned $500 into $3000 and $3000 into $9000; all about just a little micro economy that we started that we have now grown into something huge. So I teach that in *The Elegance of Living* and also I teach on sales, on marketing, or facilitate, rather than teach, actually. I have a website www.theeleganceofliving.com and als www.theantiqueguild.com.au if you would like to reach me and ask me any questions.

So, is there any other tool or question or anything like that that you would like to offer to people, that they could walk away with and start to change their financial reality, today?

For so many people I think the issue is, if you are anything like me, there's something about money, or knowing about money, that you are avoiding. For me, that's what it was. And if that resonates with you at all, I would start asking yourself, "What is it about money that I am avoiding?" "What is it about knowing about money that I am avoiding?" Because, everywhere that I had my head in the sand and was doing a great ostrich impersonation, was where I was limiting my life around money. That's a question I would start asking myself, "What about this am I avoiding?" It used to be, when I was in debt, I would hear you, Simone, and other people say the same thing and I would get *so* angry: You would say, "It's so much harder not to make money than it is to make money." And it occurred to me, if I am making it harder, obviously I am avoiding just what is laid out there for me on a plate! So what is it about having and earning money that you are avoiding? Ask yourself. It's not about you are right or you are wrong. Just ask yourself. Where you are now is not wrong.

INTERVIEW WITH CHUTISA BOWMAN AND STEVE BOWMAN

Taken from the Joy of Business internet radio show, "Getting Out of Debt Joyfully with Chutisa & Steve Bowman" aired on 22nd August 2016.

Steve, I'd love you to give me a little bit of a rundown on how you were with money, growing up. What was that like for you? Were you educated about money? Were you taught about money? Was it hidden? Ignored? Or was it something that was really out in the open and you talked about?

Steve:

You know, that's the first time anyone has ever asked me that question. This is the first time I will ever answer it. So, when I was growing up, my mother was a single mother and there were three kids, and we had quite an abusive father who was chasing us around for something like 15 or 20 years. Money never, ever came up. But it never came up in a positive nor a negative. It never came up in a judgment nor a possibility. It just literally never came up. So, I suppose, thinking about it now, I grew up never knowing what anyone else's point of view about money was.

So, when we started looking at things..., I always knew from a very young age, even before I met Chutisa, and we met when we were 16. First boyfriend and girlfriend ever, and then we got married and we've been married over 40 years now. So, the thing with that was, we always had a different point of view about money. We didn't know what other people's points of view were about money, because we didn't grow up with, or *I* didn't grow up, with any of these points of view about money. So the interesting thing to me was, when I look at money now, I'm willing to change my point of view about it, because I never grew up with one.

If there was no point of view about money, whether it was positive or negative, were things affordable or were things put to, "You can get that only on Christmas and Birthdays," or was there a cash flow that was available?

186

Steve:

The interesting thing is, when I look at my family, my sister, for example, bought into a point of view that money was always someone else's problem, not hers. Now we grew up in the same family, but you always hear or see things different. So, the thing I would say that I have learned over the years is, it's your own point of view that matters. It's not anyone else's. So, you can blame your parents, you can blame society, but that is just an excuse for you not changing your point of view about money. So, one of the things we found, for example, I grew up with no money. And, when I met Chutisa, things started to change because we started to create our life together. And, for example, we went to the U.S.A and stayed there. We lived there for two years, and we lived there on $2 a day. What do they call those dinners? Movie dinners? TV Dinners! Two dollars a night, TV Dinners. We lived on that for something like a year, a year and a half. But we always knew we could create money and we did whilst we were over there. What that gave us is the knowing that we actually can create. So, money didn't come into it. The fact that we could create did come into it.

You said that when you met Chutisa, you had more of an awareness that you could create. Do you perceive that it was having somebody else around you that had no point of view about what creation was, or, what does that look like for you with another person creating?

Steve:

Again, another question that has never been asked of me! So, one of the great things about being with someone who was always being creative - not doing creative, she's actually being creative – is it brings out the creative in you, in me; it brings it out in me. So, we've always created our life from how we wanted our lives to be and the interesting thing with that is, that has also included money. One of the things I will say now, is that one of the great gifts that everyone can give to their life, and we've learned this over the last few years, is that it's never too late. It's never too late to actually create life; it's never too late to create change, it's never too late to actually change your financial reality. Every year we look at what else can we change, what else can we change, what else can we change? Even three weeks ago, we totally changed our life around financial reality in all sorts of different ways. So, the key thing in that is, if we had a point of view about what money should have been, or should not have been, then we wouldn't have been able to change that. What we find is, when we start to look at whatever the point of view about money, or about debt is, if we are willing to change that, everything else changes. We find this every year. It's not just a once-off thing; it happens all the time.

I remember when I lived in London and I had hardly any money and I had at least 50 recipes you could cook with two minute noodles. I didn't have a point of view that I was poor. I didn't have a point of view that I lacked anything. I was just willing to be aware that if I didn't spend money on buying lots of different types of food or expensive food, I would have more money to travel. Because at that time, travel was definitely a priority for me. So, my question is, when you were living on $2 a day on your TV Dinners, what was your mentality? What was the point of view that you had?

Steve:

The point of view, for us, was that we would do whatever was required to actually create more. So I was doing two Masters Degrees in Washington DC and Chutisa, out of nothing, created a very successful fashion design business that was the talk of the town in New York City; whilst we were living on $2 a day TV Dinners, and it was because we never saw ourselves as poor; we just knew that created. We had to create. And she was absolutely amazing during the two years that we were there. She would work 23 hour days to create, and actually created a very successful fashion design business; which is unheard of. And I was doing two Masters degrees at the same time, which was also unheard of, but we didn't think of that, other than, this is how we are choosing to create our life.

Chutisa, I'd love to know, what were you bought up like in regards to money? Were you educated about it? Were you taught about it or was it ignored or you weren't allowed to talk about it? What was the general vibe in your family? Now, you grew up in Thailand?

Chutisa:

Yes. I grew up in a very much, what you would classify as aristocratic family. So talking about money means you are boasting or you are being obnoxious about it, so you must not be talking too much about money. But my father is what you would call a black sheep of the family, so he would do everything that you are not supposed to do in an aristocratic family; so he got judged so badly. He thought of himself as an entrepreneur, so in that time, you're talking about 60, 70 years ago, there was no such thing as entrepreneurs. So he was judged as risky, a risk taker, doing terrible things with money. So I had experience dealing with the judgment that was projected at him and of course our family, because we had a father who was doing things against the society and against the culture that [believed] he should be working and making good money and doing the right thing. But he went out trying to create the business that wasn't so successful. So that kind of angst about money was there. Even though we had the money, the anxiety around money was huge.

When you say "terrible things", was that just a judgement because it was different? What sort of things did he get involved in that you learned about growing up?

Chutisa:

He's one of those people who had big visions. You know, if some people want to go and have a retail business, my father would look at building a whole mall. If somebody else was thinking about doing something, you know, building a garage, he was building an airport; that's what he was doing. He had capacities to get people to invest in all these sort of things. And I realised that, you know, there's two things: one has capacity to talk about money and inspire people to donate; invest. But we have to have a capacity to generate as well; to do with doing, as well. You have to be able to make it happen. I sense that that is the path he needed to have to become successful.

So, I know that Steve had something else he wanted to add here, with his lovely wife's father and how he was and he appears to be. Steve?

Steve:

Well, it's interesting. When you have a whole lot of people that judge it because it doesn't fit their reality; it doesn't fit the reality of an aristocratic family. He was brutally judged by most of the people in his family. Yet, at his funeral - we happened to be there when he passed away - were some very senior government, and somewhat shadowy, figures. And they turned up to the funeral to pay their respects, because he had created things with them and shielded them at the same time. So, he was a man that we will only ever know some of the story. But because he was so fiercely judged by the family, then it's only been the last 10 or 15 years that we have come to the awareness that maybe he actually did things that we didn't even know about that created huge change out there. So, the thing that we take away from that is, judgment killed all of that possibility.

Chutisa:

And that judgment is very true for me because I was not, until Gary Douglas, the founder of Access Consciousness, facilitated me to see that I am very cautious, and very much not a risk taker with money, and I see the connection between the fact that my dad was a risk taker and not very cautious about money; so everything large and everything huge was the reverse of what you chose. So anything that large or huge I would not choose, because I had that connection that that's not responsible with money, until Gary actually showed me that it's not the risk taker, and everything shifted in our universe. Now I'm willing to look at bigger projects.

So, interesting to say that you are not a risk taker, Chutisa. When I look at the story that Steve just told about you guys being in New York, living on $2 a day TV Dinners, and you starting this major fashion label from pretty much nothing, to me that is pretty much a risk. So, how do you see that?

Chutisa:

A risk taker with money. Particularly with anyone else's money; I never risk anyone else's money. Talking to you now I have realised that I risk my money; anyone else's money, I wouldn't. And that's linked to the judgment of..., when you are big entrepreneur and you want to create a major success out there, you have to be able to use other people's money, right? So, if you can't be a risk taker with other people's money, then you're going to always be cautious. So, you're just going to keep yourself small.

How would you advise people [in regards to risk-taking with other people's money]? What other information do you have with that?

Steve:

One of the premises of this conversation is how to get yourself out of debt, and how to get that with joy, joyfully. And one of the things that we've found is, we've had investors in businesses and the businesses have decided to fold up so we paid all the investors back, even though we didn't have to. The thing for us, behind that, is that we are willing to risk anything. We, Chutisa and I, are willing to risk anything. But, we're not willing to risk anything on behalf of other people. And that is still a limitation. It's not a right or wrong, but it is a limitation. However, we've also seen other people that just couldn't give a rats; they couldn't care what other people have given them and what they would do with that. I think in all of this is that, be aware of when other people are willing to invest in your business, be aware and be willing to make good on what needs to occur. I mean, that's just our point of view. So, the thing that makes it easier for us is that we know that we can create money out of thin air, constantly, and we do. Knowing that, how can you ever be in debt?

Talk a little bit more about that, creating money out of thin air, constantly.

Steve:

Well, there are so many ways to actually create wealth. And this is another conversation – [the] difference between wealth and riches. What we have learned in our life is, even as recently as a couple of weeks ago, just having these "aha" moments all the time. Don't forget, it's never too late! So, creating money out of thin air is just a way of looking at it, there is so much money out there, there's so many possibilities out there. They're screaming at us to look at them, yet we refuse to see them most of the time. What we have found in our life is that there have been so many different things that we are now doing that we refused to see for 5 years, or 10 years or 15 years. And now we are doing it, once we got over our points of view, then all of a sudden our businesses have increased. I have a very large consulting business; an advisory business. I had the point of view that I was the valuable commodity, okay? Two things wrong with that story. Number one, valuable. Number two, commodity. So as soon as Chutisa and I started exploring that and saying, "Well, what if we created the business in a different way so that I wasn't the valuable commodity in this particular business? What would that look like?" And, still do the stuff I love doing. And that then created other businesses. So, now we are online. We've got a range of other things. We've got other people involved. Once I got over the point of view that I had enough of staff, I had 300 staff at one stage. Enough already. Once I got over the point of view that I didn't want any more staff, the business grew again. Once I got over the point of view that I needed staff, the business grew again.

So, the basis here is getting over your point of view?

Steve:

That's the kicker.

Where can people find out more about what you are creating?

Steve:

Well, there's a range of different things. We've got a website, which is www.consciousgovernance.com. There's another one which is www.befrabjous.com which is a blog site that has all sorts of amazing stuff on it.

The word frabjous comes from Alice in the Looking Glass. It's a Lewis Carol saying which means amazingly joyful. So be that! And you'll find some cool stuff that Chutisa has written in there. There's also the luxproject.com. There's nomorebusinessasusual.com. There's also strategicawareness.com. If in doubt, do a google search on Chutisa Bowman, because then you'll find all the websites, because hers is a lot easier to find than when you google on Steven Bowman.

Steve you mentioned about how you are still educating yourselves about money. And you mentioned the difference between wealth and riches. Can you talk about the difference?

Steve:

The thing for us is that we're constantly looking at the points of view we've got on anything. So, I had a point of view, for many years, which worked for us, to a point, that cash flow was what our consulting business provided to us, and with that cash flow we could then generate and create in terms of other types of investments. Unfortunately, what that point of view did, that I only realised about three or four weeks ago, was that it stopped me from looking at other generative sources of wealth, because I was focused on the cash flow. And I was convinced it was right, for about three or four years, that cash flow. As soon as Chutisa and I had this conversation, "Well, what if there was more to wealth than just the cash flow? What if there were different ways of looking at the cash flow? What if there were things that could be created that created cash flow in a way that it wasn't cash flow, so that we could have cash flow that we didn't have to decide was cash flow?" And that totally changed then, and from that moment, three weeks ago, we created two new businesses that have already started to create a different flow of money; because I'm not calling it cash flow now.

What you would now describe as the difference between cash flow, riches and wealth?

Steve:

So, they're all points of view, first off. Wealth to us, at the moment - and it changes all the time - is the willingness to create and to generate from that creation. Now, we'll invite Chutisa in a moment, because she's very erudite when it comes to looking at wealth. Cash flow can be very seductive, but can also take your eye off the creative game as well, too. So, yes it can be important, but it is not the end game either. And I think I had misidentified cash flow as the end game.

Chutisa, how do you see the difference of wealth, riches, cash flow, etc.?

Chutisa:

Well, the word "cash flow" already has some funky energy for me all the time. It just took me, like Steve said, until about three weeks ago when I said to him, "Cash flow almost creates no choice. Once you stop working, or stop doing all this, you stop the flow of cash. So what would it be like if we looked at building assets as creative generative income, generative revenue?" And, when you talk about generative revenue, it just keeps on generating more revenue, right? So it's a different energy to "cash flow". Because cash flow, I connect to linear. We are "baby boomers". Most people of that era, our colleagues, are going to retirement, and Steve often says, "I will never retire. I will work forever". Can you feel that? He is already setting himself up that he will work forever, right? So, I said "Well, that is a different choice to, 'we have so much generative wealth that we will choose to do the work, to be the contribution to make the world a better place forever.' It's different to 'I will work forever so I can have the cash flow'".

The cash flow... there is not much choice in that: "you must have a cash flow". But if you have generative wealth, that keeps generating itself.

Steve:

One of the great keys to this is to educate yourself in all of these possibilities. Now, as soon as I say educate yourself in these possibilities, I can hear "Eek!" going off in people's universes. Education can be as simple as getting on to google and doing a search on YouTube on how can I... yada, yada, yada, whatever it might be. Even if you googled something like, "What is wealth?", "How do wealthy people get wealthy?" and read it through your own points of view and choose the one or two things in there that actually make sense to you. Because that at least is a start. We found out three weeks ago that there were areas of wealth that we never considered before, but they've always been there, screaming at us, but we refused to see what they were. And as soon as we realised what those things were, we started putting it into action and all of a sudden, we're now making $1000 a day, $2000 a day in areas that we could have always done, but we never thought of that. That's over and above everything else that we are doing.

Chutisa, what have you got to add about the whole educating yourself about money? What would you offer people to start to educate themselves?

Chutisa:

I think the key question is, when you hear the words "educating yourself", it's not like you're going into financial planning 101 or anything like that, or getting an accountancy degree. It's more like, find one thing that is fun for you and just learn as much as possible about *that* particular thing. Like we said about jewellery. If you like that, learn everything about jewellery. It could be antiques, it could be gold, silver; just start with one thing that is fun for you and learn as much as you can and be in the question about what would it take for me to make money with this? You can buy and sell, or you can do design. You can do all kinds of things. It can be a huge financial training to be with one thing that makes your heart sing and just go and learn about that. Educate yourself, and then add more. Keep adding more.

I was wondering if you could talk about how you see the difference between debt and demystifying the judgement that most people have around debt and being in debt?

Chutisa:

Well the thing that people call bad debt is, they use other people's money, like the bank's money, and buy consumable goods, and the goods don't actually expand and grow money for you. You can create a good debt by taking money, getting a loan from the bank for say 5% interest and use that money to generate 20-25% on that money. So that is a better way of using the debt; the good debt.

Steve:

The thing with debt always is, that if you are using other people's money, which is the definition of debt, to create an asset that is going to then create revenue for you, then why would you call it a debt. If you're using a debt, that is money that you owe other people, to create something that you are going to consume, and it is not an asset that will create money for you, then that is the debt that you want to stay

196

away from. So again, the thing is, get rid of all the things where you are consuming, using other people's money, but look at ways you can use other people's money to create assets that then create new money.

For people out there who are thinking, "How can this apply to me? I've got, college debt, and I've got all this debt sort of rolled up," what do you recommend? What questions, basic tools, just for people to start to change that, to start to get out of that funk of thinking that this is their life, that there is nothing that can change?

Steve:

It's never too late to start, in any of this. And it's never too late, whether you are 20, 30, 40, 50, 60, 70, 80 years old. It doesn't matter. Because every time you change, then that changes your life as well too. So, some practical advice on this. This is not financial advice, by the way. This is just practical advice. Is to look at ways that you can reduce the amount of consumable debt that you have got, where things that you are looking at to consume. Look at your credit cards as ways of actually purchasing assets that will create revenue. Now, what are those assets that create revenue? Do a google search that says, "where are the assets that create revenue?" and start to look at the ones that will actually make fun for you. And start looking at how you can then use some of your money that you are creating in other ways, to then generate some of these assets; even if it's only $1000 a month, or $500 a month. It's more than anyone who is not doing $500 a month. And you start, well you start; and it is absolutely the best way to start is just by starting.

I think using the example of the silver spoon is brilliant. If you want to buy a silver spoon, educate yourself on what the price of silver is. Buy it below that price and, therefore, you could always, if you wanted to, melt that silver spoon and still make more money than what you paid for it.

One of the things that has really amazed us over decades is that if you educate yourself on anything, that means that you will know more than 99.99% of all the people out there. You see, people only know what they know, and if you know a little more about something, then immediately you can see the value in things that others will not see. So, using the silver spoon. Read a little bit about silver. Get on there. Do a little half hour course on YouTube, for nothing, about "How do you value silver?". Then look to see, do another search on "Where can I buy a silver spoon?? You buy a silver spoon below melt value. Then do another search on "Where can I melt silver?" You melt it. Then you've made an extra 20% more than what you made before. Now, if you did that three times a week, just imagine!

Is it bad that I went, "Oh no, don't melt the beautiful silver"? Steve, but I am the one who will buy it off you so that you don't melt it; there's always a customer somewhere!

I have heard you talk about profit a lot, about maximising profits.

Steve:

Well, one of the issues always is, we find that a lot of people would rather have 100% of nothing than 20% of something. And if you've got the point of view that you want to maximise the amount of profit you are going to get from something, you just won't, because you are always looking for the *best* time to sell it, for the *best* price; for the top dollar on whatever it is. What if you were actually really comfortable knowing that you just created 25% more than what you had when you first went into it? and what if you did that constantly, constantly, constantly? How much do you think you would generate in a year, if everything you touched you were then able to sell, or sell on, for 25% more? Not 300% more, not 500% more, but 25% more? Most people would rather wait 3 years and sell something for double its price than to sell something for 25% more, 10 times a year.

Steve, is there anything else that you would like to offer for everyone?

Steve:

I would just like to invite everyone who is listening/reading this, to get out there and start looking around at what is freely available out there about creating and generating wealth. And just pick one thing. If you picked one thing, then you would be ahead of 99% of the population. And this is one of the great gifts of getting out of debt, is to change your point of view. It's all about getting out of debt. What if it wasn't about getting out of debt? What if it was about generating assets?

Chutisa, anything else that you would like to add?

Chutisa:

Put aside a percentage of your revenue or income. No matter how small it is, it will accumulate. And just use that money to buy assets that will generate more income for you, or more revenue for you. So start small. Keep it. Put aside and use that money just to buy generative assets. If you like silver spoons, put aside money and just buy one silver spoon when you can afford to get one silver spoon. And that in itself will be more generative for you and for your life.

INTERVIEW WITH BRENDON WATT

Taken from the Joy of Business internet radio show, "Getting Out of Debt Joyfully with Brendon Watt" aired on 29th August 2016.

How did you grow up with money? What was your family life like with money? Did you talk about it, not talk about it, was it hidden, not hidden, did you have it, not have it? What was that like for you?

I remember growing up and I used to ask my parents, "So how much did this cost?" and they'd say, "None of your business." And then, I'd be like, "How much did this cost?" Everything I'd ask about money, their response was, every time, "None of your business. You don't need to know about that." So, growing up, I pretty much figured that money was, you know, something you'd avoid, something that was non existent, and in my early years of adulthood, it was something that showed up a lot. I remember I'd get bills in the mail from power companies, or phone companies, or whoever it was, and I wouldn't open the mail, because I figured that if I don't open the mail, then I can't see that I owe a bill. So I could just avoid it. Or, if a private number came up on my mobile phone, or my cell phone, if I didn't answer it, then I obviously couldn't owe any money, because I didn't know anything about it. So I avoided it, and avoided it, and avoided it, till it came to a point where I owed that much, I was in that much debt, that it was really time I had to look at it.

Can you tell me about what that created for you? What are you aware of now that you weren't aware of then?

I remember one time, when I was sharing a flat with a friend of mine. He was away at the time and the power bills must have been coming in, but I obviously wasn't opening the mail, and the power went out, so I ran a power-cord from one of the power points outside; because it was a block of flats, they had power points outside that weren't anything to do with the flat. And I ran it into the unit and plugged everything in. I didn't think it was a problem, I just thought "Great, I've got power again". And he came home from this trip and he looked at me like, "What are you doing?" and I was like, "Well, the power went out and I don't have any money to pay the bill." And I thought it was completely normal. Like, I had grown up with poverty and poverty was a real thing for me. It was just like, it wasn't wrong, it wasn't right or wrong, it was just, "I don't have any money, so what else am I going to do? Of course I'm going to run a power-cord from outside." But that is what it was like for me.

So, you actually got creative.

Yeah. Well, I needed power. I needed some way to keep the fridge cold and the lights on. But that's what it was like for me. I didn't even notice I was in debt; I was that uneducated about money. Debt wasn't even a thing for me. It was just, "I have no money." But I remember the time when we… Simone and I moved into the first house that we got together, and we were talking one day and I bought up, "Oh, by the way, I've got $200,000 worth of tax debt." And she was like, "What?" and she was like, "Well, that's kind of a big deal" and even then I was like, "Really? It's a big deal that I've got debt?" But once again, I didn't realise that debt was a bad thing, or anything; it was just money and money meant nothing. I was never educated on it, so therefore, I had no respect for it.

Yeah, I remember having that conversation with you and I was like, "We bought a house together, we are living together, isn't that the sort of thing you tell someone before you do that? That you have that much debt?" and you were like, "Oh". You treated it so casually. We did laugh about it.

Yeah, but that's what money was to me; it was, "Oh, I forgot about it." I learnt to avoid it that well that I kept it from myself to a capacity that few people could; I was good at it!

One of the things that you said to me a while ago is, when you grew up, people around you fought about money. I remember you said you never wanted to have money, you never wanted to have anything to do with it, because to you it equalled a certain level of abuse and violence. Can you talk about that a little?

Yeah, exactly. You know, I see that for a lot of people. For relationships, for instance, if someone grows up with abusive relationships, either they get an abusive relationship so they can try and figure it out and do it better than their parents did or, say with money for instance, if money was something your parents fought about, then why would you wish to have it? You know, because for me, I tried my hardest to make my parents happy. I was always in question of what could I do to make them happy? And they were fighting about money all the time, so obviously I couldn't do anything about money to make them happy, but it wasn't a cognitive thing. It was something that I decided, somewhere along the line of "Well if this is what money feels like and is then why would I want to have it?"

You also mentioned happiness. As a child growing up, did happiness equal money, money equal happiness? Or was it just irrelevant? How does that work?

Well, for me happiness had nothing to do with money. The way I defined happiness was being on my own, or doing something that made me happy. What kids do you see that create their lives based on money; create their happiness based on money? They don't go, "I earnt $10 today, so I am happy." They go, "I had a great day today, so I am happy". But as adults, we seem to go, "I didn't earn any money today, so I am stupid," or "I had a shitty day," or whatever it is. "I can't be happy, because of money". So, how many people have decided that money equals happiness? Because it doesn't. I mean, I thought that. Once again in my younger years of adulthood, I thought, "If I could make more money, I could be happier," but I realised once I started making money that it was irrelevant. Happiness was a choice that I needed to make and it had nothing to do with the money, at all.

Is there any particular moment in your life that you could say started that awareness?

Well, I mean, I met you and I met Gary and Dain and I met a lot of other close friends that I have now, and a lot of them have created a lot of money, and it's not that it's created happiness for them, or me now, it's more the choices that it gives you. Like for us, for example, I love to fly business class and I love wearing nice clothes and I love eating nice food, and I love all that stuff; that makes me happy, and it makes my body happy, but it's also a choice that I need to make to have that. It's not just, well if I had $1000 right now I'd be happier. Because, if you gave me $1000 right now, it wouldn't create happiness. It would create, "Ooh, I have $1000 right now. Awesome."

You mentioned choice. That money gives you more choice. For example, you travel economy, you travel business class, or …

Well, what's going to make you happier? Economy or business class?

What's going to make your body happier? Definitely business class or first class!

Or private jet.

Or private jet, which we have flown a few private jets in the past few months; which has been a lot of fun. So, we're talking about choice. Did you actually feel like you had choice growing up with money, or no choice? What was that like for you?

For starters, I didn't know what choice was. For me growing up, choice was looking at what everyone else chose and thinking, "Okay, is this what I should choose? Is this what I should choose? Is this what I should choose?" Not, "What can I choose and what choices do I have here, available right now?" It was never about that. It was looking at what I could choose for someone else, or against someone else. So, learning about choice was probably one of the first steps in being able to create a different reality with money. And the debt thing as well. I had to look at it and go, "Okay, I am in debt. This is not going away." So, I spent the last 30 or 40 years running away from this. This is at my doorstep now, and it's knocking. And it's still knocking. And it's still knocking. I need to open the door and I need to look at this. And I did; and that was, that was only two years ago. It was two years ago that I started realising how much debt I had accumulated and, "Now, okay, so what choices do I need to make to get out of this?"

What was it like when, the first time when you took hold of your financial life and knew that you were the one who had to make it different; that you were the one who had to make some more choices?

I was fortunate enough to have a lot of good friends around to bounce things off and say, "This is where I am at". But I also surrounded myself with people that had money; so I educated myself. I thought, "If I'm going to get out of this...", the first thing that came up for me was, "I'm going to need to educate myself about money." So, for me, that was, spending time with people who knew about money. That could be, you know, watching the finance channel. It could be reading anything to do with people who actually have created education around money, and who are educated with money. And, it was just educating myself, and then I could look at, "If I need to get out of debt, I need to do this, this and this. What are my choices? What do I need to choose here?" And then, "What feels lightest?" And go for it. And I did and, that was a couple of years ago and it's completely turned around. I mean, I don't have any debt now, apart from mortgages and things that are making me money.

Tell me about the difference between when you first used to go to the accountant and now. You never felt great when you walked out, and now you love having financial meetings or tax planning meetings with our accountant. What's the difference in the creation?

Well, the difference is, there is no avoidance of money. If I had the point of view that I needed to avoid debt and avoid money, then how could I speak to an accountant? It's not that easy to talk to an accountant when you have a point of view that money sucks and, for me, it was getting over that and changing that point of view of what I had around money. Now when we meet with our accountant I'm like, "Now what do we do? What can we do with this? What can we do with this? And how do we put this there? And how do we save tax here?" It's just exciting, because creation is exciting again and not about creating more debt. Now it's about creating a future and wealth.

So, how did you change your point of view, Brendon? Can you give us, say, three tools or questions?

My number one tool would be the 10% account. Straight up. Number one. If you can do that, you'll get out of debt. And, the reason being is, if you can put away 10% of everything you earn, straight away; if you earn a thousand dollars a week before you go and pay your bills or whatever it is, you put $100 into a separate bank account, or keep it as cash in your drawer or your safe, or whatever it is and don't touch it. If you earn $1000 a week, and that's $100, in 3-years-time, how much money would you have? You'll have $15,600. So, if you have $15,600 sitting in a separate account, will you feel like you have money, or not have money? Will you feel like you can create money or not create money? For me, I did it probably five times and I'd get to 2 or $3,000 and I'd spend it. Then, I said to you, Simone, "This isn't working. I really want to do this. I really want to change my money situation." But that was the demand I had also. "Can you hold this money for me? Can you hold my 10%?"

And you said, "Don't give it back to me, even if I ask for it".

And I think I asked for it a couple of times.

You did. And I said, "No." And you said, "What?"

I was like, "Damn!" So, that was probably two or three years ago and I haven't touched it since. So it's built and built and built and built. And now, I have a certain amount of money in the bank, so I don't feel like I don't have any money.

Can I ask you, what amount of money was it that you required to have in your 10% account before you felt like you had money?

I think at the start it was like $10,000. And then I hit that amount and it was like $30,000. And then it goes to $50,000. But once you get to the certain amounts it's like, "Oh wow. I have money. Now what else?" So that was my first thing. And that would be my number one tip on getting out of debt. My next thing would be writing down your expenses; everything. I mean, we do ours every few months, and we put down Christmas presents on there; a monthly thing. So, we know when it comes to Christmas, we might spend $1000, $2000, $3000 on Christmas presents or Christmas lunch or having family stay over, you know, that's an expense.

I remember we worked out one year that we spent $8000 on Christmas. So instead of going, "Oh, $8000 at Christmas" we divided it into 12…

And put it on our monthly expenses.

Can you tell us more about how you work out monthly expenses?

Okay, if you are old school, write it down on a piece of paper. If you are new school, Excel spreadsheet; which I hate, because I can't use them. Simone's just… oh, I can copy and paste like nobody else! But, do up a thing and say, "Car: car registration, car petrol," whatever. " House: rent or mortgage." Then you've got water, you've got electricity, you've got kids, you've got school, you've got clothes. And then you've got you. You've got clothes, you've got whatever it is, but every single thing you spend money on, you need to put that in there, because that's what you run your life with. That's what your body requires. So, put it all down, as a monthly thing or a weekly thing, whatever it is for you, and then look at it and for example if you earn $1000 a week, you do your expenses and it's $1500, is that really going to work? You are $500 down. Rather than going into a freak out and going, "Okay I need to cut down on my expenses. I need to cut down on how I live my life. I need to stop having as much fun. "I can't go out to dinner anymore," look at, "Okay, so what do I need to add to my life now to create that $500 and more?" Look at what you can add to your life, rather than what can you take away from it.

The first time you did that, do you remember the amount and what that was like for you?

I don't. I have no idea. But I think it was… I couldn't tell you the amount, to be honest, but it wouldn't have been much. I remember it was definitely over what I was earning; it was well and truly over what I was earning. Hence where the debt was coming from, because I had no clarity on what it took to run my life. Using the $1000, for example, if I was earning the $1000 a week and then I did my expenses and it was $2500, if I kept going into debt more and more and more, but I didn't know why. I just thought it was poor management, or the universe … God hated me, "God. Why don't you love me?!" But I had no education there, so when I put it down I went, "Oh. That's why I am going into debt. It's because I am not making enough money to cover my expenses." So it created absolute clarity for me. I went, "Okay, cool. I'm $1000 or $1500 down a week on what I need to be earning." So you have choices. You either cut all these things out of your life that you love doing, or, "Okay, what do I need to add to my life today that can make more money? What else can I create? What other revenue streams?"

What other tools and questions did you use to change your debt and generate money?

Questions are a valuable thing. You need to ask questions, because the universe will provide. It's not a linear thing. For me, I grew up with it as a linear thing, but once I started asking questions, I realised, I could ask for something and it would start showing up. You need to walk your talk to a certain degree. "Ask, what would it take for this to show up?" And have trust in yourself that it will. Have trust in the universe that it will. Because that's what it was for me. I knew my life would change and I knew that if I asked questions and I started making different choices it would. I didn't know how, but it did.

Also ask, "What do I hate about money?" "What do I love about not having money?" It might be confronting because you'll go, "But I don't hate money. I love it, but I don't have any." If you don't have any, you don't love it. And that was the one thing that I had to be brutally honest with myself about and go "Wow, there's something here I don't love about having money." So, ask yourself that and be willing to look at it and acknowledge, "Wow. That's a weird point of view. What would it take for me to change that?"

Another question you could ask is, "What am I not willing to do for money?" because a lot of people have these things where they'd do this, this and this for money, but if you truly desired to have all the money in the world and create everything and have everything it is that you desire, you need to be willing to do whatever it takes. And that was one of the things that I got. And another thing that I looked at, was, I need to have that amount of demand in my world. If I am going to change my life that much and have money in that way and I'm going to have everything I desire, I'm really going to be needing to do whatever it takes. One thing I see with a lot of people is that they are not willing to do what it takes.

So, talking about doing whatever it takes to create something... The first time you went to America was flying economy. The first time you flew all the way over from Australia to Italy, which is quite a trip, it was in economy. And then now you are travelling in a private jet. Did you ever think that was possible?

I always knew that was possible. But the funny thing was, the first trip I made to America was for a 7-day class in Costa Rica. I had $10,000 in the bank, saved up. And I was like, "I'm going to go to America and I'm going to travel business class and I'm going to go to this class," and I was looking at business class tickets and they were going to cost me $6000 return to America; so I had enough to do that, with the class. And I was like, "Cool." And then I looked at it and it was like, "Why would I choose that? I have $10,000 right now. I could get an economy class ticket for $1000, do the class and I would still have $5000 to either do more or create more, or have a little bit more freedom with money." Because one thing that I know about money is, when you have it, you have more freedom to create more. I can create more with it than I can without. So I looked at it and went, "Wow. This is crazy!" I had this weird point of view that if I could look like I had money, then I would make more money. Or, if I could fly with this business class ticket, then I could act wealthy for a 13-hour flight, or whatever it was. For me, looking at that was, "Okay, I need to be a little bit more pragmatic here with a), the way I look at money and b), the way that I spend it."

You actually had choice though. You could have chosen to spend all your money and do that and yet you chose different.

I did lots of economy trips when I started. I knew I wanted to travel business class, and I'd walk on to the plane and I'd see these people in business class and I wouldn't go "Oh, look at those people; you know, rich people". That wasn't me. I'd walk on the plane and I'd be like, "I'm having that. Whatever it takes. What is it going to take for me to have that?" I'd go and sit in my seat. Enjoy the flight. I started saving up miles with different airlines and I'd get upgrades. And then I'd get upgrades into business class and I'd go, "This is awesome! This is what I'd like my life to look like. What's it going to take?" Sum total, that was it, I demanded it and asked questions and that's what it took for it to start showing up.

Where do you see money coming from? And how do you see it showing up? What has changed for you in the past couple of years since you have changed your point of view around money?

Well, the number one thing is like you just said, is change your point of view around money. Because your point of view creates your reality. Straight up. That's it. If you have the point of view that I earn $20 an hour and I work 40 hours a week, that's $800, that's all you're going to earn. That's it. If you say that's what I've got, that's what I do, then that's it. Because as soon as you go to conclusion of that's the money I earn, that's what shows up in your life. But if you go, "Okay, cool. I've got a 40 hour job. I earn $20 an hour. That's $800 a week. That's awesome. That's my bread and butter. That covers my rent, my food, my whatever. Now what else is possible? What else can I create? What other revenue streams can I have?" And, once again, it's question. All the time. If you start asking questions, if the first thing in the morning when you get up you change your point of view, rather than "I've got to go to work", you function from "Awesome. I'm going to work and what else is possible?" I guarantee you, if you're sincere with that question and you're sincere with the point of view you have around "you're going to create your life different and you're going to create your money flows different, no matter what it takes", I guarantee you within six months you will have a different financial reality; I guarantee it!

When I first met you, you were a tiler - a tradesman is what we call it in Australia, and you had a business with someone. Can you talk a little bit more about how you came about to create so many more revenue streams? What I see that you create in your life too, is there's no end to it; there's no finale of how many revenue streams you have. Can you talk a little bit more about that?

Well, first thing I looked at was, I used to work really hard 5 days a week, or 5 and a half, or 6 days a week, and then I'd be like, "Oh cool, Sunday's here," and I'd lie around and watch TV or drink beer or do whatever. I remember, when I met you I'd do the same thing, but it got to a place where I looked at it, and I started looking at my life and looking at whether I had enough in it and whether I was truly happy with what I was creating, and I realised I was not. I was bored shitless. So I looked at, "Okay, what else can I add to my life?" and that's what I look at now: do I truly desire to go and… ? We have money. I could go home and literally relax. I could just go home and ride the jet skis and chill out. Would that work for me? Not in a million years. I need to do lots of things. If I'm creating my life, I'm happy. If I'm sitting around I'm not. It's awesome going and riding the jet skis or whatever, and it's not enough for me. I knew that having a 9-5 job wasn't enough for me. I knew that sitting around drinking beer on a Sunday wasn't enough for me. Not to say that it can't be for you, but if it isn't, then you need to look at it. First question is, "What else can I add to my life?" That's what I look at every day, "What can I add to my life today?" Rather than, "I'm too busy" or "I can't do anything else." That's a lie. Move forward. And when you get to, "Well I'm too busy," or "I don't want to do that," ask, "Is this really my point of view? Or is this someone else's?"

One thing we have added to our lives is a stock portfolio. What was your point of view in the beginning and what did you have to change in order to create a successful, a very successful, stock portfolio?

Well, stocks excite me because there's something about making money that quickly that excites the hell out of me. I mean, I remember going to the TAB when I was 11 or 12, which is the gambling place in Australia, where you go and put money on horses. My dad would give me $1000 cash and this list of horses he'd want me to go and put it on. I'd go down there and I'd put it on and I'd go and collect his winnings. Well, either he'd lose all the money and then be this abusive asshole, or he'd send me back down there and I'd pick up 3 or 4 grand and I'd be like, "Oooh, that was easy." So I had this thing about making money quickly that was fun for me. And it was the same with stocks, "Wow, you can make money that quick by literally, using your awareness?" And that's what I love about stocks, it's like, "If we buy this, will it make me money? Yes? No? Yes? Yes? Okay, cool, let's buy it."

Well, we actually had this stock portfolio that did so well, that we ended up selling a bunch of shares and buying a house on the river in Noosa, Queensland; which is not a cheap deal.

We bought this stock; it was very low. It was a penny stock and we bought a lot. Well we actually bought it when it was high and we bought it when it was low, but we bought a lot when it was low and recently it went up a lot, because we knew it would. We kept buying it and we kept buying it. Everyone kept telling us, "You're crazy. You're crazy. You're crazy". Our accountants would tell us. Our friends would tell us. Family would tell us, "Don't do it. You're putting all your eggs into one basket." What did we do? We kept buying it. Why? Because we knew that it would go up. So, my point is, what if you went with what you know is going to create your financial reality, instead of what other people tell you?

So you'll go to your accountant, for instance, and they'll say, "Well you should do this because it's safe," or you should do that or you should do this. What is it that you know about money that no one else does? Or what is it that you know about money that you are not willing to acknowledge? So, what if you asked yourself this, "What do I know about money that I am not willing to acknowledge?" And, "Okay, so what do I need to do to put it into action?" It's like, "Great! Universe, you've given me this awareness about what I need to know about money, now what?" Ask, "What is it going to take for this to show up?" "What do I need to do?" "Who do I need to talk to?" "What do I need to institute for this to come to fruition?" You need to make these demands of yourself. That's what you are going to need to do if you want your life to change.

One of the things that Access has taught me is that I know things. I don't think about them to know things. I don't read a book to know them. I just know them. So if I'm asking questions and I ask, "Okay, so what do I know here about this?" and then something pops up for me, "Okay, cool" and then I go in that direction. Rather than, "Well she said to do this, so I'll do that. Then they said to do this so I'll do that." No. Ask people questions to get information, not answers.

Brendon, I am very, very grateful that you joined us today. Is there anything else you would like to add before we finish?

One other thing I want to leave with is: money follows joy. Joy does not follow money. If you are willing to have joy in your life in regards to everything, including money, money will follow that. If you were having a party and you invited money and you said there's going to be no drinks, there's going to be no dancing, there's going to be no laughter, there's going to be no fun allowed, do you think money is going to want to come to that party? So what if the party you were inviting money to was about, "Hey, let's have some fun together." If money was an energy and you were willing to invite it into fun, would you have more in your life or less?

INTERVIEW WITH GARY DOUGLAS

Taken from the Joy of Business internet radio show, "Getting Out of Debt Joyfully with Gary Douglas" aired on 5th September 2016.

Gary, you are one of the most inspirational people I have ever come across with the way you look at money, the point of view that you have had about money, the point of view you have about money now, the place that you're always willing to change it and, of course, you're the founder of Access Consciousness. So, all of the tools that we talk about here came from you, and you assisted not only me, but hundreds of thousands of people to actually change their point of view about money. So, thank you for that.

Thank you. And, I had to change my points of view about money in order to be able to get it.

Can you tell us a little bit about how you grew up? What was your family life like? Did you have money; were you educated? What was that like for you?

I grew up in the "Leave it to Beaver" age; and that's not 'get laid a lot'. That's, you get to talk about things but you don't get to do much. I grew up in a middle, middle, middle, middle, middle, middle, middle, middle class family, where when the furniture wore out, you'd get rid of that one and buy a new thing to replace it in exactly the same spot and nothing ever changed; it was always the same. You used your rugs until they had a line in them and then you would exchange them for a new rug. And they wouldn't turn them around or change them or do anything with them; everything went to the same place and stayed in the same place. And, when I was growing up, my mother told me at one point, she said in front of me with somebody else, "I don't think Gary will ever have money because he'll give it all away to his friends." Because I would get 50 cents for my allowance and I would take it and I would go buy my friends pie and coke and stuff; in those days, they were really friggin' cheap. You could buy a comic book for a nickel (five cents). So that gives you an idea of the difference in things. So 50 cents was a lot of money in those days. I would get 50 cents and I'd go and I'd spend it on getting pie and coke for my friends, as well as myself, and I was interested in having a good time. And my mum said "You will never have more money if you don't get serious and if you keep spending your money on other people". I went, "But it's fun!"

What was she trying to teach you at that time? Was it about more saving money?

It was always about saving for a rainy day, but she and my father had grown up during the depression, so from their point of view, you have to not spend money, you have to take care of what money you had, and you had to always cut costs as much as possible, and you never go beyond the boundary of anything; you never choose anything greater than that. The funny part about it is, my father was a little bit of a gambler, so in 1942 when I was born, we lived in a place called Pacific Beach in San Diego, and right up the roadway was a little village called La Hoyer; which is now one of the most expensive areas of San Diego. My dad had a chance to buy a square block in what is now downtown La Hoyer for $600, and they had $600 in their savings but my mother wouldn't let him do it. My mother would always say, "No, no. You have to wait until we have more money." And it was always about waiting, for everything. And she believed you needed to wait before you create.

So what was a typical dinner time at the Douglas house: were you actually allowed to talk about money at the dinner table?

No, no. You can't talk about money. That's crass! You don't talk about money. The funny part about it is, the people who have money, their point of view is "You can't talk about money because it's crude," right? Why is it crass if you're poor or crude if you're rich? I don't get it. Neither one of them is good. It was so interesting to watch my family do this. My mother would make salads for us...and she would put a piece of lettuce on the bottom of the plate and then she would put a piece of pineapple circle in it, but she'd cut a little tiny piece out of each circle and squeeze them together and then she'd put a dollop of mayonnaise in it and then she'd shred some cheese on top of that, and that was our salad. And she'd get a little can that had three slices of pineapple and then make four salads out of it by taking a piece out of the other three, in order to make sure that we had four salads, so that we had something to eat. I kept going, "Why?" And then she would feed me things like broccoli and I'd go, "But I don't want it." and she'd go, "There are starving Chinese children. You eat every bite." And I'd go, "Can I send it to them?" I got whooped for that one!

When you were growing up and you were surrounded by this energy of "playing it safe"... you said your parents lived through the depression; with all of this going on around you, was there anywhere where you bought into their point of view? Or did you always know you were different? What was that like for you?

One of the things that was always interesting was that we'd go around and, at Christmas time, we'd go out to the rich people's section of town and look at their beautiful Christmas trees; because they would have picture windows and stuff and they'd have these fabulous trees in them. And we'd go around and look at them. Today you'd go around and look at the lights people put on their houses. You'd go, "Wow. That's amazing that they can do that." And I'd go, "Can we have a tree like that? Can we have a house like that?" and they'd go, "No honey. Those rich people aren't happy anyway." I thought in my head, "Can I try it?"

So, was the general consensus when you grew up that happiness wasn't about having money?

Oh, money didn't bring you happiness. You know, my mother said, "Money doesn't buy you happiness." I said, "What does it buy?" I'd like to find out what I can buy. And she would say, "You can't afford it. You can't afford it. You can't afford it." Everything was about what we couldn't afford. It wasn't about what we could afford. And for entertainment, because my parents were so poor, entertainment was going out and looking at rich houses on Saturdays and Sundays; open houses. I'd walk into a house and go, "Oh, I love this house. Can we have this one?" "No." "I love this house. Can we have this...?" "No." "I love this..." "No." Why are we looking at these things? If you can't have it, why are you looking at it? And my point of view became, why look at what you can't have, unless you can figure out a way you can have it?

Were you born with your own point of view about money? When did you start to change your point of view around money and know that you were different?

Well, number one, I realised I don't want to live like this. I had a rich aunt and she lived in Santa Barbara and we used to go and visit her. She had fine china and she had crystal glasses and she had sterling silver flatware. And all of this was normal for her. Instead of going to the store and buying some pastries that were $1.79, she'd go to a bakery and get six pastries for $6. And I would go, "Oh my god. I want to live like that!" She listened to opera and had such an elegance of living. I demanded

"You know what? I want to have this kind of life. This is the way I want to live. I want to have beautiful music. I want to have beautiful places I live in. I want to have beautiful things to eat off. I want to have beautiful furniture." In my family, if it wasn't utilitarian, you didn't need it.

I was always startled at the things my parents would not ever be willing to spend money on. In my younger years we used to have double feature movies, they would send me to the movies for 25 cents and that was babysitting for them, so they could have a good time without me. And they would send me with my little sister, by myself, and it would be a double feature cowboy western movie. And the two of us could have one little bag of popcorn and one little coke, because that was all we could afford. For special treats, we'd get an extra 10 cents, so we could buy junior mints, once a month.

When your mother mentioned that you would never have money because you spent it on your friends, I get it was [not so much about spending money and] more about the generosity of spirit that you function from... you'll always gift anything you possibly can. You have no limits with that. How important do you see generosity of spirit for someone to actually create more money in their lives? What effect does that have?

One of the things I noticed is, when I gave my friends the pie and the coke - probably because of the sugar - they got happier, number one, but number two, they always then would give me things that they had at their house that they thought I might like. At the time, I was totally in love with comic books. So they would always give me the comic books that they had already read. So I didn't have to spend money on the comic books. I would still get the comic books, but I would give them pie and they would give me comic books, and I ended up getting more comic books than I would have gotten if I spent all my money instead of spending it on pie.

Gary, one thing you talk about in Access is the difference between giving and taking and gifting and receiving. Can you talk a little bit more about that?

I noticed, if you truly gifted something and you don't have any expectation of anything, then things come to you from odd places in other ways. One of the things I noticed when I gave my friends that pie is, I would get things from them but I would also get gifts from other people. I mean I had neighbours, granted I was probably really cute, which I was, but the neighbours would give me special gifts all the time. I would do things for them, like if they'd send mail to our house instead of theirs I would take it to them; things like that. But they were always giving me little gifts because I was so generous with my time, my energy and my smile. That was all I had to give in those days; I was a little kid, you know? I was 8, 9 years old. You don't have much to give but that. And so, if you gave what you gave because it was what you had to give, people would give more to you than you got by not doing it, and I began to realise there's something else other than my parents' point of view.

The only time I saw my father worry, who was always generous, was when he saw somebody who didn't have enough to eat. He would always give them food, even though we functioned as though we had no food. But, in our house, there was always a dessert. There was always meat, potatoes and a salad and a dessert; and you got that every meal. And, my mother had grown up on a farm, so that was her perspective about life.

My father had grown up where his father had left his mother and he went out with a gun, he found a way to buy a .22 and he took that gun and he went out and shot rabbits to feed his entire family. And his father had left his wife and 6 kids to fend for themselves, and so he hated his father. And he went out and worked himself to death, basically, and he did that so we would not have to do without food or that we would not have to suffer. And I thought it was quite amazing because my uncle

218

went to college, my aunt went to college, but my dad never did. But he was so busy feeding the family, he never studied. He was exhausted at the end of the day. He was a great athlete and did really good in that kind of stuff, but he never learned how to create money. From his father, the only thing he got was the awareness that you have to take care of your family and you have to feed people. And that was sum total of his point of view about money.

So, I sort of came away with that point of view and when I had a family, that's what I wanted to do most. But I also realised, "Wait a minute, I managed to create more money by being willing to be generous." And I watched my father be generous to people who had nothing, and I watched them come back to him with a gift of kindness and caring and loving that I didn't see other places. My parents were really quite remarkable. I'm really pleased by the fact that I got to have them as parents. My mother was kind. My father was kind. They didn't do any terrible stuff to us. They didn't beat us; I think I got whipped 3 times in my life. They tried to take care of us and they tried to do the best that they could for us and they wanted us to have a good life. And, that's the one thing that I realised, that few people recognise about their parents. They look at what their parents didn't give them. And they don't look at what their parents did give them. And I really got that my parents were doing the best they could with what they had. So when I went to my aunt's house, I went, "I want to live like this. I don't care what it takes, I'm going to live like this."

One of the things I see is people continuously buy into the point of view that their parents / grandparents / the people they were bought up with had around money, rather than actually asking some questions about what their financial reality could be. I can see how you sort of embraced what they gifted you and yet you still created your own point of view; you still created your own perspective around money.

Well, I started asking questions early on. "How come I can't have that?" "Why? Why? Why?" As my mother used to say, "Could you please stop asking questions?" "Okay. Why can't we..." I could be quiet for about 10 and a half seconds.

Nothing's changed. I'm still that way. I'm always asking questions. And I was always asking questions then, because I looked at things and I went, "Why is this the way it is?" I watched my friends say, "Well, you can't have that. You can't do that." And I'd go, "Why?" and they'd go, "Well, because you can't." I'd ask, "Why not? All you have to do is do this; I've done it." And they'd say, "Yeah, but you can't do that."

"Why not?" I questioned. I grew up in the time when questioning authority was big. But I had grown up in a bigger time where I questioned everything.

What are some of the pragmatic, practical tools you could give people; any questions, favourite questions or tools, to start creating their own perspective around money?

Well, one of the first ones I came up with for myself when I was a kid was, "Okay. What am I going to have to do to get the money I need?" I started asking that. The only thing I can think of was my parents must have tried to instil in me a work ethic, because they both worked constantly, so they must have. So I said, "So what can I do to make money?" and it was like, "Okay. You can mow lawns." And I wasn't very big; I was a skinny, scrawny kid and I would go to neighbours and ask, "Can I mow your lawn?" And they'd go, "Sure. How much are you going to charge me?" "Whatever you want to pay me." And some of them would pay me one dollar and some of them would pay me 50 cents. And I figured, "Yay, I've got 50 cents. Yay, I've got a dollar." I was never looking at what I should have got. I didn't have that conclusionary reality that most people have: I should have made more, I should have gotten more, I need more. I went, "Okay, I've got this. Now what?"

So, more coming from the place of gratitude?

Yes. I was grateful for the fact that I got things, and I noticed that gratitude when I gave my friends pie; there was a gratitude in them that contributed energy to me and my body that I didn't feel other times. And, I didn't feel that when I saw people working and doing things, and I really wanted that.

The other thing that you speak about, that I would love to get your thoughts on, is using money to expand people's realities. When did you first come to the awareness of that?

Well, that was actually much later in my life, because, I had literally gone through the period of "Oh yeah, like I'm a hippy and I don't have any money," to, "Okay, I'm going to be a drug dealer and I'm going to have money." So I grew pot so I had lots of money but that didn't make me happier either. I noticed that the people that I knew who had done a lot of drugs ended up in jail and I went, "You know what, I won't go there. So, I think I'll stop this." I've worked for various people and I did everything I could to do it right, to do everything right, and whenever I was generous in a strange way, something magnificent would happen in my life. I remember, I was in my twenties and I went to work for this riding school and I was riding horses. And there was a lady there who was as rich as god, and she had a beautiful thoroughbred horse that she showed, and she was elegant and drove a really nice car. I made five dollars a day plus room and board. So, she's out in front of her stall of her horse sitting on a tack box crying and I said, "What's wrong?" "I'm broke. I have no money. I'm so out of money, I don't know what I am going to do." I said, "Well, can I take you out to dinner?" So, I took her out to dinner, and we're sitting there at dinner and the dinner is $25; five days work for me. And, she gets up to go to the bathroom and her cheque book falls out of her purse onto the ground and it's open and it shows that she has $47,000 in her checking account.

I went, "Holy shit! Wait a minute. Her idea of broke was less than $50,000." After a while we had a conversation and I said, "So, I saw your cheque book. What makes you think you're broke?" "Any time I'm under $50,000 I know I'm broke. I have to have $50,000 or I'm broke." I went, "Well, that's cool." And I realised for me, if I was negative $100 I was broke.

So everybody has a different perspective.

Yeah.

The book that you wrote with Dr Dain Heer: "Money Isn't The Problem, You Are" - all of those tools in that book literally got me out of debt, because I started to change my point of view around money. One thing I see that is so imperative is that you need to change your point of view. You need to change how you look at money, how you be with money, and how you start to educate yourself about money.

That was the most important part. Here I was with this lady who has $47,000, and a $20,000 horse, and I can barely afford anything and I have to live in one room in a club house and I earn $5 a day, but I was doing what I loved. I realised she was spending lots of money to do what she loved. I was making little money to do what I loved. I went, "Okay, so what would it take to have a different reality?" I started to question that: "What would it be like to have a different reality?" I wanted to be like her, where I'm creating my money so I can spend lots of money to have fun. I want to have fun, but I'd like some money as well, and that's when things started to change for me. I questioned "Okay, you know what? This has to change." And, that's the one thing I think you have to do, is look at your situation and demand, "Okay, enough! This has to change." And just taking that one stand for yourself, because that's what it is; a stand for yourself. Just taking that point of view; and that's what you did Simone when you said, "Enough. I'm getting out of this debt." It's like you take a stand for yourself and then the world starts to adjust itself to what you need. It's remarkable.

So I've heard you when you say the world starts to adjust itself. And it's one of the things that I heard at the beginning and went, "I have

no idea what you are talking about." For anybody hearing about this for the first time, can you talk more about, "the world starts to adjust itself"?

Well, Dr Dain Heer and I bought a ranch recently. I went to Japan and I ate Kobe beef for the first time and I went, "Oh, I've got to get more of this. How do I get more of this?" and somebody said they only breed that certain kind of beef in Japan. And then I found out that they had them in some countries like Australia, so I asked "I wonder if I can get those in America?" So I had a friend go online and he found a place in America where he could find them and he found seven cows for me. And I went, "Wow, I love having these cows. These are so pretty." And they are beautiful black cows. They are kind and gentle and they're just amazing critters; I kind of hate to eat them.

I had this guy go out and buy these cows. Five days later he called me and said, "I just found seven of these cows"; and I'd just bought seven. "Seven more cows for only $6500." And I went, "That's less than $1000 a cow. I'll take them."

What I see with that, Gary, is you continuously create. You're not actually looking about the riches or the wealth it's creating, you're looking at what you can create.

Yeah. And I figured, worst case scenario, I can eat for 8 years. You know, I've got 8 years of beef on the hoof...

A lot of people don't think that they can have riches, they don't think that they can have wealth. I mean, I've heard you talk about when you had to live in a very, very small bedroom with your son and eat nothing but cornflakes.

It wasn't a bedroom. It was a closet. I lived in a closet, literally, in somebody's house, with my son sleeping next to me on a foam mat. My clothes were hung on one end of the closet and I lived on the other end and I had no money and all I could afford was cornflakes and milk;

because that's all my kid would eat at the time anyway. I was paying $50 a week to live in these people's closet.

And then what sort of demands did you make for yourself?

I went, "You know what? Enough. I'm not going to live like this again; not ever again. I don't care what it takes. I'm going to make money. I'm going to get money." Right after that everything changed. I had always loved antiques but I had gone to this antique shop to sell something that I had. And, I said, "Wow, your shop has some great stuff, but you could really use some reorganisation." The woman looked at me and said, "Do you know anyone that can do it?" I said, "Yeah. Me." "How much do you charge?" Ummmmm, "$25 an hour." It was like that was way more than I was earning at the time, and it was like, why not? She said, "I'll pay you $35 if you do a good job." "Done." So I went in and rearranged her shop and the next day she sold like five things that had been in her shop for two years that were bought by two people who had been in her shop numerous times in those two years. And they said, "Oh, is that new?" I said, "Yes!" And they said, "Oh, I think that would be perfect for my house." The thing I learned about advertising is, you need to move things around so people see them different. Because the different light will create a different effect on them. And look at your life that way; "What do I have to move around in my life to create more; to sell myself better, to create more money, to have more possibility in life?" It's really amazing to see it happen when you finally start to ask those questions of, "How can I arrange myself and my life so that I appear different to different people who are then going to want to purchase what I have to offer and listen to what I have to say?"

So, again, that's like changing your point of view around money, continuously. And also, doing what you love. Because you love to work with antiques. It's like you probably would have done that job for free.

Well, I had done it for free, which is why I knew I could do it.

Throughout your life then, you've obviously had different amounts of money that you've earnt. I see a lot of people go, "Oooh, I have my house now – tick," and tick that box. Or, "I have a car," and they tick that box, and they seem to stop creating. What can you tell people, or what tools can you give people in order for them to not have that limit?

The main thing is that you've got to look at whether you have a goal or a target. The one thing I found long ago is that the word "goal" meant a jail. If you make a goal and you achieve it and you don't acknowledge it, then what happens is you go backwards in order to be able to achieve the goal you think you haven't achieved. So, I went "Wait a minute. I'm not going to do goals. I'm going to do targets." So I would make a target and as soon as I achieved the target I could always shoot another arrow and get a bullseye again. And for me I went, "I want to be able to constantly change." Changing is a thing that is most important for me in life and without change, there is no creation. If you really want to create your life, start changing.

And with that change, when you are in a continuous place of change, the money shows up. Wealth shows up.

I know. It's weird.

Can you give an explanation of how you see the difference between wealth and riches?

Wealth is accumulating those things that other people will buy from you for some amount of money. Riches is when you have enough to spend anything you want.

If you really want to have wealth, you want to surround yourself with things that will be worth more, no matter what. If you want riches, you want just enough to be able to spend and buy what you have decided you want. Everybody I know who has gone for riches, they buy all these things and then suddenly they have no desire for more, because they're not actually trying to create wealth, they are trying to create riches.

13

Once you recognise, "Wait a minute, wealth includes things that are valuable to others. What is valuable to another, that they would pay you for it?" And when you have that in your life, then everywhere you walk, everything you do is about the wealth of life, not about the riches of what you can spend.

So it's making life not about money, it's actually making it about what we've been talking about; the generosity of spirit, the creativeness, the willingness to receive, the willingness to gift?

And allowing yourself to be generous to you. Because most of us are not generous to ourselves. Whenever you judge yourself, you are not being generous to you. Whenever you see you as wrong in some respect, you are not being generous to you. You want to be generous to you. And it's not about how much money you spend on yourself; it's about how well you take care of you.

Most of us think we have a problem with something, but we don't. It's what we invent in order to keep ourselves doing the thing that's limiting us and keeps us in the place where we belong. And that's one of the things I realised about my family is, they wanted to keep themselves in the same place. They had a small house and everything was controllable. It was always about the control of it. And I wanted to be a little out of control. I wanted to be doing something different. And so I started creating difference early on, and it was a very amazing change in life to realise that I could have something different and I could choose something different. And I did.

I got that you have to look at things different, and one of the things you've got to do is look at, "What's right about this and what's right about me I'm not getting?"

For example, the other day when we were out horseback riding and somebody ran up behind your horse and your horse started to spook, and I asked you today, can I give you some information about what happened then? And I said, "Look, you've got to get that horses have the point of view that when another horse is running up behind them they're going to be required to run too. So they start getting ready for it. You sat there on your horse and you controlled him and he did not run off. Do you get that that's not a wrongness? That's a brilliance of ability? Because most horses try and run because the other horses are running. You didn't let him run. You got him under control." You did a brilliant job and then you felt shaken and you felt like you were not good and you got off.

Talking to you today and watching you ride, I could feel your trepidation about riding him as though he might do a similar thing. But I want you to get that you had actually done a beautiful job with that animal. The thing about horse people is, they seldom tell you that you did a good job. And it's like, you know, I love horses, but I'm not that fond of horse people, because most of them don't tell you anything good about what you did, they tell you what you did wrong. And I said, "What you've got to get is that was friggin' brilliant." And you sat there, and you sat tight on him. You weren't going to fall. Nothing was going to happen. And this boy loves you so much, he'll take care of you. You ask him when you get on to take care of you, and he always does.

I am so grateful for you talking to me about that. And I realised, how often we don't push forward with ourselves; we don't demand more of ourselves. Instead, we get off the horse and go, "that's okay."

You get off your business.

You get off your business. You stop creating money. Because what? You lost money? Something happened and you're in the red; you're in minus? It's like, so what? What if now was the time to change it?

I've filed bankruptcy four times and you know, I hated it. But I decided, "Enough." And the real changing point in my life for my monetary situation was when I was 55 years old and I had to borrow money from my mother to keep from losing my house. And prior to that I had let my wives run the money, and I went, "Enough. Never again am I going to have to borrow money from my mother. This is ridiculous. I am too damn old for this to be a reality." And, I got to work and I started creating money, and I've been creating money ever since. And it's been phenomenal. And it's like, I will not wait. I will always create. I was waiting for my wives and I was waiting for my partners and I was waiting for everybody to deliver something. I don't wait for anybody now. I get out there and do the work, now, for me. Because I honour me. You need to honour you because guess what? When you do it right, do not look at what you did wrong, but what you did right. Always ask, "What's right about me and what's right about this I am not getting?" and you will change your life; it's not hard.

Even when I [Simone] was in debt, I still created and you never would have been able to tell that I didn't have money. And now that I have money, it's a very, very different energy. Can you talk about the energy that changed for you when you actually had money, and have money, and what does that create for you? And the planet?

Yes. I love it down here in Costa Rica. And I have horses here and I bought horses here. I got to the point where I realised that every time I was interested in a horse, it became double the money. It was always twice as expensive if I liked it. So I kept trying to get other people to buy for me, but it never worked. One of the people, Claudia, who does a bunch of stuff for us in the Hispanic community, said to me, "Do you realise you're rich." I go, "I'm not rich." She said, "You're rich." And I go, "I'm not rich! I don't have millions of dollars in the bank." "You're rich." And I looked at it and went, "Oh, I earn a lot of money, that makes me rich in other people's eyes." It's like the lady who had $47,000 and I had $5 a day. Her idea of rich and my idea of rich were different. Not wrong. Just different. So, you've got to ask, "What can I change here? And if I can change this, how do I create my life different?"

Thank you for that question. We have one more minute, is there anything else you would like to tell people out there in the world?

Go out and create. Don't wait.

If you hold on to money tightly enough, you will lose it. It's a guarantee of losing it. You can't hold on to money, you can only create with it. Money is a creative force in the world, not a continuous force in the world.

INTERVIEW WITH DR DAIN HEER

Taken from the Joy of Business internet radio show, "Getting Out of Debt Joyfully with Dr. Dain Heer" aired on 12th September 2016.

So, the idea here is I wanted for people to actually get that this is not just me, Simone, that has been in debt and used Access Consciousness tools and changed stuff. There's a lot of people out there who have changed their point of view around money and changed their situation with money, including yourself Dain.

I've got to tell you - from the time of first meeting you - having you as the Access Consciousness worldwide coordinator as I started becoming a co-creator of Access - it was so interesting to me that you actually enjoyed what you were doing. I grew up in a family business and they hated it; they hated business. They really actually hated money, except for my grandfather who created the business. I left that experience with some really strange, fixed points of view.

What I wanted to start with is exactly what you were talking about. How did you grow up around money? Were you rich, poor? What was your situation around money growing up?

Most of my young life - the formative years until about 10 - I actually lived in the ghetto with my Mom. When I say the ghetto, let's put it this way - the amount of money we had was like this: our toilet broke at one point and we had to wait almost a month in order to get a plumber out there because we couldn't afford it, and I'm not going to tell you what we did in the meantime. Let's just say we emptied what we should have put in the toilet, in the backyard every morning. Hey, going back to olden times. Maybe it was like our castle, I don't know! So there was that and then on the other side I had a family that actually had money, that was wealthy, but they would never contribute it. They would never give it to me or my mom to make our lives easier. So, it set up these really weird points of view around money.

Were you educated around money? Did you have any? Were you allowed to talk about it?

I actually started working from the time I was 11. I worked in my grandfather's business and I worked in the warehouse and it's like, what can an 11-year-old kid do? Everything! I mean, I just organised the place. I helped clean. I just did whatever was required. It was a great and amazing experience, and what happened was I worked all summer, and I developed several hundreds of dollars. And I was so excited that I carried it with me everywhere I went. I had it in my bag. We were going to the river where my family – my Dad and my Stepmom - used to vacation, and my Stepmom saw it there. She saw these thousands of dollars, because I would cash my checks and I would hold it in cash and I was like, "This is awesome!" I didn't spend it then, because I loved having money. And, she went into my bag and took it and said, "A child this young should not have money." I was 11 or 12 at the time, and it stunted my willingness to have money from that point forward. I mean, I obviously have changed it since, thank God.

But it really created this place in my world where I was really conflicted and confused about money; as though I shouldn't have it. As though it was a bad thing. And it was one of the those defining moments in my life where money became this really weird thing for me. Whereas before that, it was easy. It was like, "Yeah, I'll go to work." And, literally, I was working, don't tell anybody, but I was working probably 30 hours a week at 11 years old. It was with my grandfather, so that was acceptable and all that. But there was a lot of confusion that used to exist in my world around money. And then when I got to my teenage years, my family that had money and had the family business, the business failed because they weren't willing to look at the future and choose according to creating the future.

My grandfather who created the business was getting tired. He was also getting tired of supporting my uncle and my father, who basically thought they were entitled to whatever money he had. And, so the business failed, literally. And it's interesting, because both sides of my family the poor side, which pretty much grew up in trailers and different parts of the world, and the "wealthy" side, were defined by money. And when my grandfather's business failed and the money was lost, oh man! That was the most trauma and drama that you could imagine. And it went on for years! The fact that they had lost all their money and they couldn't create more money, and they couldn't create the business that they wanted to... Talk about utter confusion.

Can you talk a little bit about the confusion? I still see, no matter what confused you, you have still managed to create your own reality around money.

I think a lot of us out there, we actually have our own reality around money that's different than our family, that's different than what we grew up with, that's different than our boyfriends and our girlfriends and our husbands and our wives and the people we grew up around and our friends. But we've never even taken a moment to acknowledge that. And to acknowledge the difference of that but also the greatness in that. And that for me, is huge. I was always willing to do whatever it took to create what I wanted. I was willing to work as hard as I needed to or as much as I needed to. And, in that, I finally found... and you and I have been on this journey together, and I know you've seen a lot of the places where my paths sort of kicked in to create limitation... but it's interesting to see now where me stepping into my own reality regarding money and finances is actually starting to move things forward at a really dynamic rate.

Can you give an example of creating the limitation and how you changed it to create your own reality around money?

So the side of my family that never really had any money, anytime they did get some, they would lose it, they would squander it. It's like they would invest with some guy who said, "I have a machine that's going to create free energy. Give me $10,000," and it was like, "Well I have $5.

Let me get all my family together and they can give me their savings," and they would find ways of getting rid of what little money they had.

I functioned in a different way. I liked having money and would save it. I would put 10% away and to the best of my ability always made sure I had money. But everything my family was choosing did limit my creativity so dynamically. It limited my willingness to jump off a cliff when there was a possibility available.

I functioned like this in Access until recently. And, so one of the things I want to let people know is, chaos and order exist. Neither one is wrong. Be willing to embrace the chaos potential and the chaotic possibilities that can be had with money and stop trying to do so much control of everything.

And one thing I noticed is you are pretty much willing to do anything to make money.

Yes. Might as well try it you know? The worst that can happen is you fail, you lose all your money or the thing doesn't take off. And we've tried thousands of things in the last 16 years. Especially with Access, because it's so different to what's in the mainstream, that you've got to try as many things as you can because the mainstream stuff doesn't work for us. Which is an amazing gift.

I'm reminded of Richard Branson. He looked and went, "Well, there's the main stream, and this other place over here is where I am going." Look at what he's created. He's created waves in the world of every single industry he's ever chosen to go into; or at least the ones that we know about. There are probably hundreds of ones that he's tried to go into that didn't actually work and he's like, "Okay. On to the next thing." And I think that's one of the really big things that you need to get is, "Okay, if this doesn't work, something else will." Do not give up. Never stop. Never quit. Never give in. And, don't allow yourself to be stopped by anybody. And what's so vital and essential is that you start getting *your* reality around money. And, for me, one of the things that I realised was when I changed the word "money" to "cash", somewhere in my world, that made more sense. And a lot of people talk about money but they have no idea what the heck it is. And so, for me, I started going, "Okay, rather than money, what I am going to start asking for is cash. I'm going to start asking to create cash." Now does it show up in dollar bills and that? No. Not necessarily. But when I put it in terms of "cash", for me that is something more tangible; it's not just blips on a computer screen and it's not this weird nefarious concept that I bought from a very young age, and so it gives me a different possibility. And, for me, that feels a lot more creative.

One of my favourite sayings, which I quote continuously, Dain, is when you said, "Money follows joy, joy does not follow money." So, can you talk a little bit more about that and how you first came to that recognition?

I don't even remember where I first came to it. I do remember being in a car with four of my poor family members, and we were driving in this car that really needed work but nobody could pay for it and we were driving behind somebody in a Mercedes; a convertible Mercedes. I looked at that car and it was so funny because the moment I looked, in my mind I went, "That's friggin' awesome. I cannot wait to have one of those one day." I was probably a young teen at that time and turned to one of my family members and said, "That car's awesome." One of my aunts quickly said, "Dain. Those rich people aren't happy." I looked around the family I was living with and looked at how unhappy they were and thought, "Um... It couldn't be any worse than this..."

What I started to realise in my own life was the days when I was depressed and unhappy and didn't want to get up, no money came. I recognised it when I was a chiropractor. If I was depressed and unhappy, if I didn't have the energy of life and living and enthusiasm for being alive, which, by the way, was why I became a chiropractor in the first place, I wanted to bring this energy to people. And if *I* didn't have that, I noticed nobody

234

wanted to sign up for care. People were like, "Why would I want what you're having?" Right? And so, what I started realising is, truly, money follows joy. The happier you are, the more money you are going to make.

It's interesting because we all know lots of people who have lots of money who are so unhappy. I look at that and at this point I am so friggin' blessed. I pretty much travel business class and when I'm lucky enough, first class, wherever I go because that's joyful for me. And what I've noticed is that even when I didn't have the money for it, when there wasn't an ease to pay for it, I still did, because it brought me so much joy. I *knew* it was bringing more money in; I could feel it. And I think we all can and I think we've cut it off since the time we were little kids. But one of the things I noticed is... if you're out there and you're struggling with money, or you just don't have as much as you desire, maybe one of the missing elements is the joy in your life; and maybe one of the missing elements is the joy that you have with money and with cash, like we talked about before.

One of the things I noticed in travelling in business class is how many people were angry, were pissed off, were totally superior or total assholes and pretending like everybody should kiss their ass because they had money. They weren't being happy. They weren't being nice to the flight attendant. They weren't grateful for the fact that they get free drinks. And I looked at that and I went, how does this exist? These people have what everybody else desires, supposedly. They think they have what everybody else desires, which is the money, but they don't have any of the joy to go with it. And it's interesting because I've seen so many people like that and I don't get... I mean I get it, because I've seen it so much and I get that that's the way so much of our world functions. But in reality, for me, it's like truly, the money is not about the money. I love what Gary Douglas said in one of the first classes I did with him. He said, "Look, the purpose of money is to change people's realities for the greater." and I went, "That's so cool. Finally I've got somebody who actually has a similar point of view."

Can you talk more about changing people's reality with money? What does that look like?

I was always trying to do that, even as a little kid, you know? When I was a kid and I would have money in my pocket and there'd be somebody begging on the street, and if they weren't just doing it, if it didn't look like they were just doing it to fill their pockets; if they really had a need in their world, I'd be like, "Here's 10 bucks," and this is back in the day where 10 bucks was like a billion. You know, back then; like back in the day! When 10 bucks actually meant something. And I would give it to them because my sense was, "Here, it might change your world. I don't know." And the funny part was, every time I did something like that and gave them $10, I would get at least 10 back.

I remember one time, where I was walking down the street. I had saved up this money and I had, like 20 bucks, and I was going to buy this candy that I wanted, and there was this toy that I wanted and there were like 25 things that I was going to buy with my 20 bucks. God! Remember those days? Anyway, here I am and there was this guy who came up and you could feel the need in his world and he said, "Hey dude. Do you have any money?" And I'm not even a teenager yet. And I went, "Huh." And I get a big smile on my face and I said, "Sure. Here you go." And I was like, okay I guess I'm not going to go and buy my candy and my toys right now. So I started walking back home. I literally turn the corner and there was a $20 bill on the ground. And I thought, "Wow. This is awesome." And so, the thing that the joy gives you is this sense of the magic of life and living. It truly can show up like that, and most of us have forgotten it, if we had it when we were little kids. But if you can get back to that, money shows up from the strangest places.

And this is the thing that I think is so vital that we get, it's not about the amount of money that you have. It's about the joy that whatever you do with it brings you. And that's the same thing with me. I had 20 bucks. I gave away my 20 bucks, you know?

There's such a generosity of spirit in that. Can you say more about generosity of spirit and what that creates?

It's interesting because when I first met Gary Douglas, it was like, he didn't have a huge amount of money. We would go somewhere and do something and you would have thought that he was a billionaire because of the generosity of spirit that he had. And this is the thing... the generosity of spirit you can have with money and with cash and with gifting. And also, the way you are in the world is another way you can bring money and cash to you, because what happens when you have that generosity of spirit it's like, you're open to gift, and what we don't realise is, gifting and receiving occur simultaneously. Most of us have tried to exclude them. We tried to put it into 'gifting' and 'receiving', or 'giving' and 'receiving'. Or, what most of us actually have as our point of view is 'give and take'. And I get that that's the way the world functions, but it's not the way you have to function.

And so you, me, pretty much the entire Access team, we have this thing that is a generosity of spirit, that brings us joy to gift something to somebody else. It gifts us joy to see somebody wearing something wonderful that they look great in and go, "Damn baby. You look hot today!" Boy or girl; it doesn't matter. But what that does is, that actually creates an energy of receiving from the universe itself. And when I say the universe, I don't mean the airy, fairy 'the universe'. What I mean is, we are all part of the fucking universe, you know? And so, it's not just the universe that gives you your cash. It comes through other people and through other places and that creates an energy where that inflow can continue to occur because of the simultaneity of gifting and receiving. It's not actually a give and take world; we just created it that way.

You talk about how you had two different families; one who didn't have money and one who did have money. The energy of both of those were different. What's the difference you noticed?

Basically, what it was for me, the family that had no money had this pride in poverty, and I see a lot of people having that.

Pride in poverty is one of the biggest things I see people who continuously reject money have. It's like, "You don't know what I've been through. You don't know how I have to suffer." And it's like, you don't have to hold that crap in place anymore. What is the value of that? Just because your family had it, doesn't mean you have to.

Now, with the side of the family that had money, they were penurious also; they just had a nicer lifestyle. Except for my grandfather. He was the one who created the business in the first place, who actually created huge amounts of cash and money that my Dad, my uncle, my grandmother and the rest of the family later spent and dwindled down to nothing. The recognition of that changed my world because he had a generosity of spirit and he was willing to gift continuously and he always got more.

Can you tell me a little bit more about your grandfather? What was the business and how was he with that?

My grandfather had an inherent generosity of spirit. And, as I was growing up, I handed in my report card one day and he went "Okay" and he handed me back $600. This was when I was in high school. And I had these big eyes, because I like cash, right? I love money. I'm like, this is awesome. This is so cool. And my eyes got really big and I asked, "What's that for?" And he said, "For all the A's you got." I got 6 out of 6 A's. and I'm like, "Really?" He's said, "Yeah. And every time you get an A I'll give you $100 bucks and for a B I'll give you $50." Guess who got straight A's all the way through high school?

And, you know, it's so interesting. You don't really realise sometimes, what affected you in life until somebody asks you to tell the story about it. It's happening right now. I'm going through a lot of things where I realise that a huge amount of the financial reality I am able to have right now is from what I saw him being, that nobody in our family gave him credit for and nobody acknowledged as greatness. He truly had a greatness in this area. And so, that one thing, that generosity of spirit was just amazing to me, but also just the willingness to give away cash, give away money and it wasn't like, give it away to do something not useful. He knew when it would change somebody's reality. He had the same point of view Gary does.

What he did with that first report card in high school, was show me something that I actually wanted to work for and choose and I literally got pretty much straight A's. There were probably two B+'s I got in high school. But everything else was basically really good grades. And that was part of the motivation but I wasn't just doing it for the money. I was doing it because somebody was actually acknowledging me with this gift and seeing me and seeing that it had value. When I would bring home my report card to my dad and my stepmother they would look at it and go, "Oh cool. I'll sign it to prove that I've seen it" and there was no energy. No "Wow Dain, great job. We could never do this." So what my grandfather did, made me reach for more, and once again, that's one of the things we can do with our money - contribute it to people so that it allows them to reach for more.

Are there defining moments where you had the awareness of what the energy around money can create or doesn't create?

It's interesting, because my grandfather's family business, he called it Robotronics, and people would always call and go, "Do you have robots?" And he'd say, "No, we don't really do that." They sold in serviced office machines. But he saw a need that could be filled at a very young age, created this business when nobody else had a business doing that, had all kinds of large clients, large banks, large institutions all back in the day when you used typewriters and copiers and that sort of thing. Well, as it started to evolve into the computer age, he wanted to get into it and my uncle and father who sort of had an interest in the business at that time were like, "No. We can't do this." Blah, blah,

blah. They weren't willing to see the future. That's another thing my grandfather had. He was willing to see the future, and look at what his choices would create business wise and personal wise and do what he could to create the greatest result.

And, I see a lot of people who, number one, don't realise they have that capacity, and I think a lot of that is because they are stuck in their family's financial reality. But the other thing is, at one point, my uncle actually created a business like Kinkos, which is at least in the United States and I know it's in lots of places in the world. Kinkos is basically a one-stop office, if you need to rent space, if you need a copy machine, if you need copies made, if you need banners printed, blah, blah, blah. My uncle actually created that about 15 years before Kinkos came along, but he was so committed to not having money and so committed to destroying himself, proving that he was right for his fixed points of view, that it failed. Now, you can say he was before his time. He was. But also, if he had the drive that my grandfather had, you would be talking to a multi-billionaire right now, because he actually created that concept before anybody else in the world did.

So many people get stuck in their family's point of view. For you, did you buy into it? Did you create your own reality? How can people get out of what they are stuck in with their family's point of view?

Looking at all of these things financially, I see where a lot of points of view came from, both good and bad, or both expansive and limited, but then the other thing that is actually really imperative, is now going beyond it all, going beyond all the past. It's like "Cool. I had this from my mom's side of the family. I had this from my dad's side of the family. I had this insanity over here of the poverty. I had this insanity over there of the unwillingness to have the money when they had the money and losing it and destroying it, but you know what? What would I like to create today?" Yeah, I got all this, and what I would suggest that people actually do is go back and write down all the greatnesses that you learned from the people around you when you were growing up about money. What awarenesses did you get that you've never really acted on; never acknowledged were there? And also what are the limitations? And, go down that entire list and do it 10 times, 20 times, 30 times, until you look at it and you no longer have a charge on it. Because, what's really required is not just looking at our past and reliving it and looking at it and going, "Well that's why I have that point of view. Okay, good. I'm going to go and have that point of view some more," it's recognizing that the point of view is a limitation: "Wow. That's cool. Now I know at least some part of why I have that point of view. Now I am going to go beyond it."

And I hate to say it, but my point of view about these points of view and our limitations from the past is, "You know what, fuck it!" Yes, I lived that. I experienced some horrendous abuse when I was growing up; physical, emotional, mental, and having pretty much everyone around me hate me, for a lot of my life. You know, my stepmother and with the family that I lived with in the ghetto with my mom, okay, fine. Great. I lived that. Now what? Now what do I want to create with my life today? I've got this 10 seconds to live the rest of my life, what am I going to choose from here? It's not, "I have this so I need to carry this forward," it's, "There it is. Now what can I do to go beyond it?"

Is there any other sort of really pragmatic tools that you could give people who are going, "Yeah, yeah, yeah. He did that. She did that. But what about me?" Is there anything else that you can add to that to enlighten people, to empower them to choose something different around money, and around their life?

Absolutely. And I'm totally serious when I say this: buy Simone's new book! And what I would suggest is, write down this question: "What is it that sticks me most about money and cash from my past?" And, write a friggin' novel if you have to. And then burn the fucking thing. Okay? That was your past. And here's the other things that I would like you to look at, and maybe write it down if you are willing to, but, what you want to look at is: "What is the gift that me living that gave me?" You see, we keep looking at it as though it's a curse. It's not.

I have an inherent awareness of how people who have very little money function. I have an inherent awareness of their insecurities and their desires and their sense that they can't do it. Well, what's my job in the world? Facilitating people to get out of that shit. So, that inherent awareness that I got, I don't know if I could do what I do without the abuse that I experienced. I probably could, but not in the way that I do it. Not in the way that really works for me, and kind of in an intense way sometimes. And also, with the financial stuff, it's like, given what I experienced, I got a place from which I can speak that allows me to do what I am here to do in the world. And what I have looked at with the hundreds of thousands of people who have come through Access in the time that we have both been here is, that everybody has something that they are doing here. Everybody has something that their life has contributed to them being here and doing here. Once you start to get on the tail or the trail of that gift, things start to change dramatically, because you come out of the judgment of what you experienced and then you start looking at the gift of what you experienced, and then you start looking at, "Wow." And then the other question to ask is: "How can I use this to create money and cash?"

So you're actually using your childhood, the way you grew up, using the culture, the family, everything to your advantage.

Exactly. And using whatever other tools you have. If you want to write a few more things down, you might want to write down, "What other tools and gifts do I have that will allow me to create a lot of money, more money and more cash than I ever thought I could?" And write down what else you have.

Also, there's part of this thing about not taking yourself so damn seriously. You know, we do this so much and what you were talking about at the very beginning of the show, about the lightness and the doing it from the joy, and you have Joy of Business as one of your businesses, and also a book, and when I heard about that, when I saw you doing business from joy, it was about exactly that. Not taking yourself so seriously. Having a lot more fun. Do what is fun and don't take yourself so goddamn seriously and you will actually start to create more money than you ever thought possible.

People see you now and you're successful, you have money, you're known throughout the world. But that's not where you actually started out. How did you see creating your future and what was the energy that you were, that you had to be? What did you choose when you decided to actually start charging more for you, beginning to receive more money in your life for what you actually do and be?

When I started, I was charging $25 dollars a session for my chiropractic sessions, most of the people got what they were willing to pay for 25 bucks, which was like, a movie. And it was like, "Oh that was a nice entertainment. Thanks so much," and they would leave. And then came Gary Douglas, who walked into my office and said, "You're charging way too little for what you do." But I did a session on him and he said, "This literally saved my life." And I was like, "Really? Me?" Because my level of insecurity at the time was off the charts. It's been a process over the last 16 years! And what people don't realise is they'll see somebody who has a level of success or who has a level of wealth, or who has a level of anything that they think they desire, and they don't realise how long it took them to get there. They don't realise how many mistakes they made. They don't realise how many insecurities they had to overcome.

And so what I want to say to people is, wherever you are right now, start. And get this sense of, if you could put the energy in front of you of what it would be like to make maybe three to four times what you are making now and get the energy of that. And get the energy of what it would be like to travel around the world, if you wanted to. Or at least have the time and the money to travel. Get the energy of what it would be like, not just to pay your bills but have a level of wealth and financial abundance that you like and extra cash in the bank or in your mattress or wherever you keep it at home.

And also, get the sense of what it would be like to be doing something that would actually be contributing to people and it changed all the time, where you got to work with fun people and actually enjoy your life and living. And get the sense of that energy and then pull energy into it from all over the universe and let little trickles go out to everyone and everything that is going to help make it a reality for you that you don't even know yet. You know, that's an exercise in the Being You Changing The World book that I wrote. And, it really is about being you. What it is uniquely for you that would be that energy if all of these things were to show up? And then, anything that feels like that, head in that direction. And, people don't realise that, there is something that is actually going to guide them that is actually their awareness, their connection with everything that is, if you will. And what's so funny is, successful businesses people seem to do this naturally. And then a lot of them poo-poo the energetic stuff. And I'm like, "Yeah, but here's what you are doing energetically." And they go "Yeah, yeah, yeah. No. No. Don't say the word 'energy'. Thanks a lot."

But if you can get the sense of that, it starts to create you being willing to head into the future. So you pull energy into that, from all over the universe, until it gets really big, and ask the universe to contribute. And here's the thing. I hear a lot of people saying "universe" as though it is something outside of them. You're part of the universe! So recognise that this is you asking for something based on you being connected to it, and then let little trickles go out to everyone and everything who is going to help make it a reality for you. And in so doing, what you start doing is creating the energetic future you would like to have, and the weird and wonderful part about it is, all the parts and pieces of what that would be like to create that energy start coming to you. But you have to be willing to receive them when they show up.

And this is where we get into this thing where I talked about how I kept trying to order my family, so when something would show up and it was too "big", I'd be like, "Oh no. I can't do that," rather than asking a question. And this is the next thing you want to do, when something shows up, is *not* to say "I can't do that" but "What would it take for me to do this?" And this really is the functional point of view: "What would it take for me to create this?" rather than being in that mode of the insecurity of what I can't do and what I can't create.

So there are these places where you have these insecurities, or reasons, that you have created as real, or the things that you created that you look at as a mistake, but they're not really. One thing I see with you Dain, is that you continuously choose something greater, no matter what it takes.

Yeah, exactly. One of the things I see people do when a new possibility shows up is they automatically decide they can't do it before they even start. So, this is one of the places where we stop ourselves so dynamically. And, if you look at my life, I've got plenty of reasons to say no. I've got plenty of reasons to stop myself. I've got plenty of reasons why I shouldn't be able to do it. But, I've got to say, thanks to Access and the Access Consciousness tools, because that's really this amazing treasure trove of tools to change things, thanks to that, and my closeness with you, my closeness with Gary, and my friends who actually have my back and who will be there for me when I realise I have a limitation and I want to change it, thanks to all of that, it's like, my past doesn't rule my future anymore. And I think this is one of the biggest difficulties that people have; their past rules their future. A great possibility shows up and they go "No. It's too chaotic. It's too much." Well, guess what? Chaos is creation. And the thing about chaos, we keep thinking order is good and chaos is bad. Consciousness includes everything and judges nothing; which is why it's Access Consciousness that we do. It includes everything and judges nothing.

I mean, if you look at it for a moment, the internal combustion engine, you know, the thing that powers your darn car, it functions on chaos. Explosions in your engine are what drive your car. If you tried to eliminate the chaos completely, your car would not move anymore. Same thing with the car of your life. What you want to do is you want to take the chaos and order it as well as you can to create a coherence between chaos and order that allows you to move forward. And I say that and a lot of people go, "Uh, what? I don't get it..."

But this is the beauty of it: you don't have to know how it works. But you have to be willing to stop trying to avoid the chaos that shows up and the things that you think are too much and the things that you think are out of control, because maybe out of control is exactly what you require to take your next step.

So, what questions can people ask, like if they're going, "Oh yeah, yeah. This guy can do it but how can I do it?"

Ah, just recognise, I didn't know I could do it, I didn't think I could do it either, but I was willing to try. And that's what you really need to be willing to do, is go for it. You know, the worst that can happen is it won't work. Well, guess what? How many other things have you done that haven't worked? And the other thing is that every one of those things that are our insecurities and those places where we say no, are places where we are trying to order something from our past. Every single one of those. And if you looked at that and went, "Am I trying to order something here?"

Recognise that you trying to order your past is stopping you from creating your future.

What else would you like to say before we leave the conversation?

Your point of view creates your reality, your reality does not create your point of view. These tools change your point of view, so your reality shows up differently. You don't have to suffer with money. I'm with you.

Everybody can change their money situation. You've done it. I've done it. And we've seen so many people who come to Access have done it, but you have to actually be willing to do it. You have to be willing to do the work; it's not a magic pill, but it sure functions like a friggin' magic wand sometimes!

You can change your stars, truly. You can change anything. And what if you truly being you were the gift, the change and the possibility this world requires? Are you choosing to know that? Because you are that.

Lightning Source UK Ltd.
Milton Keynes UK
UKHW040326161021
392237UK00001B/21